SEA
DISASTERS

GE

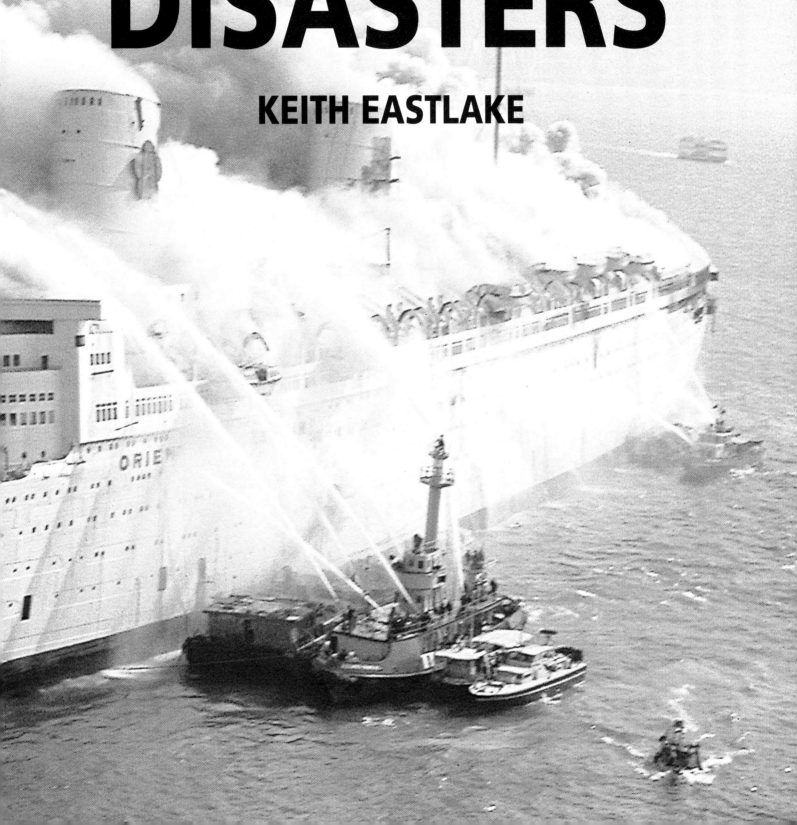

SEA
DISASTERS

KEITH EASTLAKE

ISBN 0-86288-149-8

Printed and bound in Italy

For Brown Partworks Ltd

Editor: Shona Grimbly
Design: Wilson Design Associates
Picture research: Wendy Verren
Production: Alex MacKenzie

Photographic credits:
Cover (all), Mary Evans Picture Library;
1, Robert Hunt Library; 2-3, Popperfoto; 5, Corbis-Bettmann; 6, Corbis-
Bettmann/UPI; 7t, Getty Images; 7c, Popperfoto/Reuters; 8 Corbis-
Bettmann/UPI; 9tl, Popperfoto; 9tr, Popperfoto/Reuter; 10t, Corbis-Bettmann;
10b, Corbis-Bettmann/UPI; 11, Getty Images; 13, Mary Evans Picture Library;
14, Getty Images; 15, TRH Pictures; 16, Mary Evans Picture Library;
17t, Getty Images; 17b, Mary Evans Picture Library; 18t, Corbis-Bettmann;
18b, Getty Images; 19, Mary Evans Picture Library; 20, Mr F.O.Braynard;
21, Mr A.Kludas; 22, Getty Images; 23t, Popperfoto; 23b, Corbis-
Bettmann/UPI; 24, Topham Picturepoint; 26, Popperfoto; 27, Corbis-Bettmann;
29, Corbis-Bettmann; 31, Mary Evans Picture Library; 32, Topham Picturepoint;
33, Topham Picturepoint; 34, Mary Evans Picture Library; 35, Hulton Deutsch
Collection/Corbis; 36, Getty Images; 37, Corbis-Bettmann/UPI; 38t, Getty Images;
38b, Getty Images; 39, Corbis-Bettmann/UPI; 40, TRH Pictures; 41t, Corbis-
Bettmann/UPI; 41b, Popperfoto; 42, Popperfoto; 43t, Popperfoto;
43b, Popperfoto; 44, Popperfoto/Reuters; 45, TRH Pictures; 46, Mr B.Novelli;
47, Mr A.Kilk; 48, Popperfoto; 49t, Popperfoto; 49b, Popperfoto;
51, TRH Pictures; 52, National Archives of America; 53, TRH Pictures;
54t, TRH Pictures; 54b, Getty Images; 55t, Mary Evans Picture Library;
55b, Mary Evans Picture Library; 56, Mary Evans Picture Library;
57, Topham Picturepoint; 58, Robert Hunt Library; 59t, Robert Hunt Library;
59b, Robert Hunt Library; 60t, AKG London; 60b, AKG London;
61, Popperfoto; 62t, Popperfoto; 62b, Popperfoto; 63t, Popperfoto;
63b, Popperfoto; 65, Corbis-Bettmann/UPI; 66, Robert Hunt Library;
67, Mary Evans Picture Library; 68, Topham Picturepoint; 69, TRH Pictures;
70, Mary Evans Picture Library; 71t, Corbis-Bettmann/UPI; 71b, Getty Images;
72, Getty Images; 73, Corbis-Bettmann/UPI; 74t, Corbis-Bettmann/UPI;
74b, Getty Images; 75, Corbis-Bettmann; 76, Corbis-Bettmann/UPI;
77t, Corbis-Bettmann; 77b, Corbis-Bettmann/UPI; 78, Popperfoto;
79t, Corbis-Bettmann; 79b, Popperfoto; 80t, Popperfoto; 80b, Popperfoto;
81t, Popperfoto; 81b, Popperfoto; 83, Popperfoto; 84, Topham Picturepoint;
85, Popperfoto; 86l, Getty Images; 86r, Getty Images; 87, Corbis-Bettmann/UPI;
88, Getty Images; 89t, Topham Picturepoint; 89b, Topham Picturepoint;
91, Popperfoto; 92t, Getty Images; 92b, Popperfoto; 93, Popperfoto;
94t, Popperfoto; 94b, Popperfoto; 95, Popperfoto.

Illustrations on pages 25, 30 and 90 by George Fryer

Page 1: *The Greek cruise liner* Lakonia *caught fire in the Atlantic 180 miles (289km) north of Madeira on December 22, 1963.*

Pages 2-3: *The once-great Cunard liner* Queen Elizabeth *(renamed Seawise University) fatally on fire in Hong Kong harbor on January 9, 1972.*

Below right: *The roll-on roll-off car ferry* Herald of Free Enterprise *lies capsized just outside Zeebrugge harbor. The ferry overturned when seawater entered through the open main bow door and nearly 200 people died in the disaster.*

CONTENTS

INTRODUCTION

Below: The liner Morro Castle *was destroyed by fire on September 8, 1934, off the coast of New Jersey. Here sightseers flock to see the burned-out vessel beached at Asbury Park, New Jersey.*

From earliest times human beings have ventured on to the seas in search of new lands or new people to trade with. Sailing in vessels ranging from flimsy coracles to the mighty, sophisticated ships of today, humans have been determined to conquer the oceans of the world. This had led to some of humankind's most heroic feats – and also to some of their most spectacular disasters. This book is intended to serve as an introduction to some of the disasters that have occurred at sea over the past 100 years.

The oceans of the world cover 70 percent of the surface of the globe. These oceans are a vital source of food, minerals and fuel – but they also form a natural barrier, separating far-flung lands. Sailors in the past crossed the seas for many reasons. Some, like Christopher Columbus in the late 15th century, set out to discover new trade routes to the East. Others were spurred by the desire to conquer new lands and win new territories for their own country. Some seagoing explorers simply wanted to push back the frontiers of the known world, or to extend scientists' knowledge of

Right: The French liner L'Atlantique *adrift and burning on January 4, 1933, after the ship was abandoned when fire took hold.*

Above: The car ferry Herald of Free Enterprise *capsized in March 1987 when it sailed out of Zeebrugge with its bow doors still open, flooding the car deck.*

plants animals and rock structures in distant, unexplored lands.

Adventurers of earliest times sailed off into the unknown in primitive coracles or dugout canoes – craft that to modern eyes look flimsy and unseaworthy but which nevertheless managed to cover surprising distances at sea. Later sailors, such as the Persians, Greeks, Romans and Vikings, had swift, stoutly built ships powered by sail and oar that were fully capable of tackling the oceans.

Sea-going exploration really took off in the 15th and 16th centuries, when famous explorers like Christopher Columbus, Vasco da Gama and Ferdinand Magellan opened up new trade routes and led the way to the Americas and to India. Their historic voyages heralded a great explosion of conquest and settlement. New colonies were established, settled by farmers, people fleeing from religious persecution in Europe, entrepreneurs, indentured labour – and convicts sentenced to be transported to the New World.

These new colonies began to trade with each other and, more importantly, with other countries, chiefly in Europe. This meant that many more vessels were plying the oceans, carrying trade goods back and forth. One of the most used, if most notorious, trade route of this era was the "triangular trade". This saw slave ships set out from Europe to Africa, loaded with goods to trade in exchange for slaves. The slaves were then transported across the Atlantic to the Caribbean and southern and eastern seaboards of North America where they were sold, mostly to work on sugar and cotton plantations. The ships then took on cargoes such as rum, sugar and molassses, to take back to a ready market in Europe.

These maritime trading routes were gradually extended until they encircled the entire globe. Until the advent of long distance flight in the mid 20th century, all movement of people and cargoes over the oceans had to be carried out by ships. As worldwide trade developed, the seas became crowded with more and

more ships carrying passengers and cargoes of every kind. Ships also became faster, as the age of sail gave way to the age of steam and timber-built ships were replaced by iron ones. At the same time ships became larger as maritime engineering became more sophisticated. The *Santa Maria* – the caravel Columbus sailed in to the New World in 1492 – was a vessel of 100 tons. In contrast the *Exxon Valdez* supertanker that ran aground in 1989 had a deadweight of over 211,000 tons.

All this means that as the oceans carry ever increasing tonnages of shipping, collisions and other disasters are more likely to happen. Yet the fates of the *Santa Maria* and the *Exxon Valdez* show that ships in any age can come to grief – the sea has always been and will continue to be a dangerous place. The *Santa Maria* was wrecked on a coral reef off the coast of Haiti on Christmas Eve, 1492; the *Exxon Valdez* ran aground in a channel as it was making its way toward the open seas off Alaska almost 500 years later, in 1989. Both these events illustrate the fact that the great benefits of ocean-going travel and trade come with huge costs – the loss of ships and their cargoes, the loss of life to passengers and crew, and the pollution of the oceans and their coastlines.

The history of shipwrecks is as old as seafaring itself. No one knows when or where the first shipwreck took place, but ancient history is littered with stories of disasters at sea. For example, in 255 BC a Roman fleet was returning home after being defeated by the Carthaginians at the Battle of Tunis. As the 364 ships sailed across the Mediterranean a great storm engulfed the fleet, sinking 284 vessels and drowning an estimated 100,000 Roman soldiers and sailors. Similar disasters continue to occur in every age. Our modern ships may be more seaworthy, better fitted with safety and navigational devices, and be manned by highly skilled captains and crews, but disasters at sea have not been eradicated.

This books looks at more than 50 shipping disasters that have occurred in the last 100 years or so. One in particular continues to excite and horrify our imaginations – the loss of the great passenger liner the *Titanic*. The *Titanic* was a floating palace and was supposed to represent the very best that maritime engineers and architects could create. Its loss showed that the oceans take no account of human vanities. The proud boast that the *Titanic* was "unsinkable" was shown to be just that when the liner struck an iceberg on its maiden

Above: Bodies are brought ashore from the General Slocum *disaster, in which a sidewheel ferry caught fire on the East River in New York.*

8

Above: The four-masted German windjammer Pamir *was being used as a cadet training ship when it went down in a hurricane with the loss of almost all on board.*

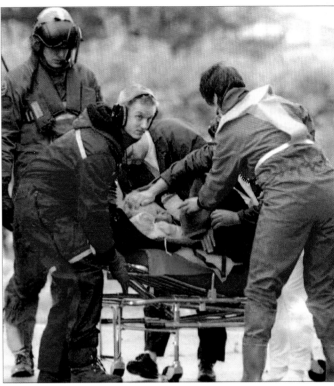

Above: *One of the first survivors from the ferry* Estonia, *which foundered in the Baltic in September 1994, is lifted from a helicopter by Finnish rescue workers.*

transatlantic voyage and went to the bottom with over 1500 passengers and crew. Although the story of the *Titanic* and the fate of those who died with the ship has been recounted in scores of books and many movies, it is just one of hundreds of disasters that have befallen vessels in the last century.

There are almost as many causes of shipwrecks as there are shipwrecks themselves. The combination of human fallibility, expensive but not always safe machinery, and the massive forces of nature have ensured that sea disasters are an ever-present danger for those who take to the high seas to trade, travel, or take a vacation. Through fire, collision, human error, mechanical failure, the weather, and explosion, ships

have been sent to the bottom. Many disasters have involved more than one of these factors.

Many of the reasons that have led to a catastrophe at sea are unavoidable. Suddenly worsening weather can swamp a vessel, a massive internal explosion can rip a ship apart, and a hidden reef can open a hull like a tin can. However, many of the ships featured here were sent to the bottom or involved in a disaster because their masters and crews made mistakes.

Some of these mistakes or errors of judgment have perhaps been understandable. It is incredibly difficult for crews to be wholly vigilant 24 hours a day; momentary lapses in concentration, for example, are unfortunate but often explicable. However, in a number of cases captains and their crews have been directly responsible for a sinking and when faced with a developing crisis have been totally unable to cope with the difficulties confronting them. In many cases, they have been unaware of safety procedures, or have not issued the necessary warnings to passengers or sent out distress calls. In a few cases they have displayed what amounts to cowardice, abandoning ship before their passengers have been evacuated to safety.

These cases are thankfully rare and, if one aspect of disasters at sea, stands out, it is the professionalism and bravery of sailors. They have fought fires with often inadequate means, overseen the evacuation of

panicking passengers with great calm, and in many cases died attempting to save their ships. Thus the rare cases of cowardice have been more than counterbalanced by tales of great heroism.

There is undoubtedly a brotherhood of the sea. Ocean-going transport, whether of people or goods, is a business in which time really is money. Delays are costly. However, there are very few examples of a ship, having seen or heard a distress signal, not responding to the emergency. Today, there are bodies such as the US Coast Guard and, in Britain, the Royal National Lifeboat Association that are tasked with rescue at sea, but they are not always immediately available. Consequently, it is often other commercial ships in the vicinity that are the most immediate source of salvation for those in peril. Many of these rescuers have also displayed great bravery in undertaking a task that is often fraught with dangers.

The history of modern shipping is punctuated with disaster, reminding us that we ignore the dangers of the deep seas at our peril. Yet we continue to have

Left: *Cleaning up starts after* Exxon Valdez *spilled oil over an area estimated at 500 square miles (1300 sq km).*

Below: *The massive oil tanker* Exxon Valdez *that went aground on Bligh Reef in the Gulf of Alaska.*

Right: One of the worst peacetime disasters at sea occurred in 1893 when HMS Victoria *collided with HMS* Camperdown *while carrying out maneuvers. Over 350 men perished.*

great faith in the vessels that sail the world's oceans. This faith is usually well-founded, but on occasions it can be misplaced, as the stories recounted here demonstrate. The loss of a ship, particularly if it involves the loss of life, is still headline news. Such events are probably newsworthy because we still find it hard to believe that in the modern world these great examples of our technological abilities can be destroyed by natural forces. Humankind cannot afford to be complacent about the dangers at sea. While constant vigilance on the part of sailors may avoid some catastrophes, others will be brought about by storm, gales, ice and fog – forces that humans are still unable to control.

COLLISION

Although on the surface the oceans of the world may appear to be flat, on the seabed the landforms are as varied as those on dry land. Under the surface of the sea there may be deep channels or dangerous reefs and shoals. So shipping tends to stick to well-defined routes that have been charted through safe waters. As most of the world's bulk goods are transported by sea, and ships still ferry passengers over both long and short distances, there are many hundreds of ships of all types and sizes daily plying their trade. Certain parts of the world's oceans are, therefore, either crowded or filled with hidden dangers.

As the accidents described in this chapter show, technology is no guarantee that ships will be immune from collision either with other vessels or with other objects such as icebergs. The *Titanic* tragedy of 1912 is perhaps the most famous collision in history, but it did not lead to the greatest loss of life. The dubious distinction of holding that record goes to the little known ferry *Dona Paz*, which sank after colliding at night with a tanker in the seas around the Philippines in 1987. It is thought that nearly 2000 passengers and crew died in this tragedy but a complete list of losses was never compiled.

Most of the collisions recorded here are ship-on-ship disasters, but they also include ships hitting reefs, icebergs, and even harbor defenses. Many occurred at night or in difficult weather conditions, proving that eternal vigilance is probably the only sure way of ensuring that collisions do not occur. However, as humans and safety devices are far from infallible, the danger of collision is unlikely ever to be totally eradicated.

Right: The mighty liner Titanic – *commonly supposed to be unsinkable – hit an iceberg in the North Atlantic on its maiden voyage and sank with the loss of over 1500 lives.*

PRINCESS ALICE, THAMES

SEPTEMBER 3, 1878

As the wreck of the *Princess Alice* shows, shipping disasters are not confined to the high seas. The *Princess Alice*, launched in 1865, was navigating the placid Thames River in London when catastrophe overtook the 251-ton vessel. Those on board were making their way to Gravesend to enjoy one of the last days of summer. For many that September day was destined to be the last day of their lives.

The *Princess Alice*, a vessel belonging to the London Steamship Company, was involved in a collision with a collier, the *Bywell Castle*. The collision and the resulting loss of 640 lives shocked the nation. One report states that it was one of the most fearful disasters of modern times – a scene which has no parallel on the river. The report went on: "the river for 100 yards (300m) was full of drowning people screaming in anguish and praying for help." Many of those on board the *Princess Alice* were families and there were many young children lost in the disaster.

The *Princess Alice* had only just left its moorings in London and had reached a point about a mile below Greenwich. Those on board could have had no warning of what happened next. The 1376-ton collier sliced right into the river steamship, which was badly holed and sank rapidly.

The ship's master, Captain Grinstead, was one of those who did not survive. When a final head count was made, there were 200 survivors.

Below: When the collier the Bywell Castle *sliced into the pleasure steamer the* Princess Alice, *many people were killed instantly. Others drowned in the river before rescuers could arrive.*

TITANIC, ATLANTIC

APRIL 15, 1912

Below: When it was launched in 1911, the Titanic *was the latest thing in luxury liners and was widely believed to be unsinkable.*

As well as being a major maritime disaster, the loss of the *Titanic* was also a highly symbolic event. The 46,000-gross ton liner was built at a time when countries gained great international prestige from these marvels of engineering. Apart from the considerable amount of money to be made from the lucrative transatlantic trade, the great liners came to symbolize a country's wealth and international status. The *Titanic* was the latest in a series of luxury liners that were intended to convince their passengers that they were as safe on sea as they would be on land. The loss of the *Titanic* was a signal that the sureties of the age were built on foundations of sand.

The *Titanic* was born when the managing director of the White Star Line, J. Bruce Ismay, decided to build three vessels that in size and luxury would outstrip anything else afloat. The first, the *Olympic*, was launched in 1909, and gave distinguished service. The third, the *Britannic*, saw action in World War I until sunk by a mine in the Mediterranean. However, it was the second ship, the *Titanic*, that was to become one of the most famous ships of all time.

All three ships were designed to carry some 2500 passengers in three classes and had crews of almost 1000. All had what were thought to be state-of-the-art safety features, including 16 watertight compartments. However, as events were to show, faith in these watertight compartments was misplaced.

The *Titanic* was launched in 1911 amid great publicity, and was widely believed to be "unsinkable". White Star planned its maiden voyage from Southampton to New York, via Cherbourg and Cork, for April 10 the following year. When the liner left Southampton, it was commanded by Captain Edward Smith.

Smith was a good choice for the prestigious first voyage. He was very experienced and been master of more than 15 of the line's ships. Despite his experience, however, the voyage began badly. As the *Titanic* left Southampton, it displaced a huge volume of water which dragged a second liner, the *New York*, from its moorings. A collision was only narrowly avoided. Although they did not know it, the 1308 passengers (who included Ismay, the managing director of the shipping line) and 898 crew on board had had a warning of the fate of the *Titanic*.

The *Titanic* stopped off in Cherbourg and Cork and then headed out across the Atlantic. There were reports of icebergs, but they were to the north of the route being followed by the *Titanic*. Ismay was eager to prove his new liner's worth, and although he had no right to do so, Ismay ordered Smith to steam ahead at full speed. The *Titanic*'s engines performed well. In the first day the ship made an impressive 546 miles (873km). Radio reports of icebergs farther to the south continued to be logged, but there was no reduction in the liner's 22 knots.

As night fell on April 14, lookouts were posted around the vessel to keep careful watch for icebergs or other dangers, and the captain went to his cabin. Shortly before midnight one lookout spotted an object ahead of the liner. It was an iceberg and he immediately reported the danger. His action was prompt but the liner was traveling at high speed. The ship's rudders were put to port and the engines full astern, but the *Titanic* was a large vessel and did not respond quickly enough. The ship struck the iceberg.

Those on board later reported nothing more than feeling a jolt and hearing some scraping noises, but the collision had fatally wounded the vessel. There was no panic – after all, the ship had been labelled "unsinkable". However, there was a fatal design flaw. The watertight bulkheads did not reach the full height of the vessel. As one watertight compartment filled, water flowed over the top and filled the next compartment, and so on. Thomas Andrews, a passenger who was also managing director of the ship's builders, told the captain the *Titanic* would sink in about two hours.

Smith ordered the sending of the new SOS distress signal and one ship, the *Carpathia*, picked it up and steamed toward the *Titanic*. It was just 50 miles (80 km) away from the liner. Help was closer at hand, however. Another ship, the *Californian*, was reportedly just a few miles away but its radio operator was off duty and the *Titanic*'s distress signals went unheard. On board the *Titanic*, Smith gave the order to abandon ship. However, there were just 20 lifeboats for 2200 passengers and crew. The builders had believed

Left: It was just before midnight on April 14, 1912, that the Titanic *struck an iceberg in the North Atlantic.*

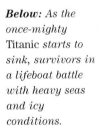

Right: After the ship struck the iceberg, some lifeboats were lowered and first-class passengers taken off. But there were not enough lifeboats to take all the passengers and crew.

Below: As the once-mighty Titanic *starts to sink, survivors in a lifeboat battle with heavy seas and icy conditions.*

that, even in the worst scenario, the *Titanic* would stay afloat long enough for rescue ships to arrive. Lifeboats would only be needed, it was thought, to shuttle passengers from the *Titanic* to the waiting vessels. This proved to be a fatal conclusion.

There was little immediate panic among the *Titanic*'s passengers. Women and children were hurried into the lifeboats, but the class system prevailed. Those who were saved were almost all first class passengers. The vast majority of those who died – men, women, and children – were in the third class. Ismay survived but Smith went down with his ship. The *Titanic* slid beneath the waves at about 0200 hours on April 15. The *Carpathia* arrived on the scene about two hours later, and picked up 703 people. The final total of the dead was 815 passengers and 688 crew.

The sinking of the *Titanic* made headlines around the world and questions were asked about how such a fate could befall such a great liner. The White Star Line was partly a victim of its own publicity – it had been so sure that the liner's safety features made it invincible. Boards of Inquiry on both sides of the Atlantic, however, pointed out a number of shortcomings. There were not enough lifeboats for the number of passen-

gers and crew carried – even though according to the guidelines in place at the time, the *Titanic* did have the correct number of boats. No boat drill had been carried out. And the ship was traveling at high speed at night in a known iceberg area.

The loss of the *Titanic* led to new safety regulations at sea. Ships were to carry enough lifeboats to accommodate all passengers and crew, and boat drills were to be held on all voyages. Vessels were required to follow a more southerly route across the Atlantic, and an ice patrol system was introduced to give advance warning of icebergs. And all ships were in future to keep a round-the-clock radio watch in case of distress signals.

Left: The scene on board the sinking Titanic, *as women and children are herded on to the lifeboats, leaving their menfolk behind.*

Below: The last moments of the Titanic *as the great ship slides beneath the water. Legend has it that the ship's orchestra continued to play as the ship went down.*

EMPRESS OF IRELAND, ATLANTIC

MAY 29, 1914

The *Empress of Ireland* was a comfortable, if unostentatious, passenger liner that was built by Glasgow's Fairfield Shipbuilding and Engineering Company in 1905 for the Canadian Pacific Line. The *Empress of Ireland* plied the Quebec to Liverpool transatlantic route, and the liner's final voyage began on May 28, 1914. The vessel sailed from Quebec with 1057 passengers on board and Captain Henry Kendall in charge of 420 crew members. The ship also carried about 1100 tons of general cargo.

As the liner reached Father Point, the pilot disembarked and the *Empress* continued on its journey to Liverpool. As the ship pushed on lights were spotted at about a distance of six miles (9.5km). They were from the *Storstad*, a Norwegian collier with 11,000 tons of coal in its holds. As the two vessels closed both seemed to believe they would pass each other with room to spare. However, as they closed, thick fog covered the area, reducing visibility. Those on watch tried to sight the other approaching ship by its lights.

The *Storstad* spotted the *Empress* first and made a desperate attempt to turn away. Kendall first ordered full ahead and then astern to avoid the *Storstad*, but it was far too late. The *Storstad* struck the *Empress*, opening up a large hole in the *Empress*'s hull through which seawater poured in.

Kendall realized that the *Empress* was finished and, after an unsuccessful attempt to get the ship beached, he gave the order to abandon ship. However, most of the passengers were asleep, and were slow to respond. The *Empress* keeled over on to its side and went under bow first less than 15 minutes after the collision. Of the 1057 passengers aboard 840 drowned, only 217 surviving. The crew were luckier – or more prompt to react – and 248 of the 420 were able to escape.

Although the loss of the ship did not receive anything like the same news coverage as the loss of the *Titanic*, in fact more passengers perished from the *Empress* than from the *Titanic*.

Right: Recovering bodies from the St Lawrence River after the wreck of the *Empress of Ireland.*

FORT VICTORIA, ATLANTIC

DECEMBER 18, 1929

The sinking of the *Fort Victoria*, a 7784-gross ton passenger ship, was fortunately not accompanied by any loss of life. However, the ship's loss in a collision with a second liner, the *Algonquin*, was a classic example of the dangers of sailing through busy waters in foggy weather.

The *Fort Victoria* began its life as the *Willochra*, sailing between the United States, Australia, and New Zealand before World War I. During the war it was used as a troopship. The *Willochra* was sold to Furness, Withy and Company of London in 1919, was refitted and renamed, and then placed on the New York to Bermuda route as a passenger cruiser.

The *Fort Victoria*'s date with destiny began when the cruise ship sailed out of New York harbor on December 18, 1929. On board were the master, Captain A.R. Francis, the crew, and just over 200 passengers. Later that day the *Fort Victoria* came to a halt at the beginning of the Ambrose Channel. Fog surrounded the ship and visibility was very poor. Captain Francis could hear warning bell and sirens coming from several directions, but nothing prepared him for the sight of a ship's bow that suddenly appeared out of the fog. The bow belonged to the *Algonquin*, out of Galveston. A collision could not be avoided and the *Algonquin* cut through the *Fort Victoria*'s hull on the port side. It was a death blow and both ships immediately sent out distress calls.

The calls for help were answered rapidly by the US Coast Guard and other vessels in the area. Captain Francis watched as all his passengers and crew were evacuated safely and then left the foundering liner. The *Fort Victoria* sank later the same day.

Left: The Fort Victoria *was a cruise ship that worked the New York to Bermuda run in the 1920s.*

DRESDEN, NORTH SEA

JUNE 20, 1934

The sinking of the *Dresden* while on a pleasure cruise illustrates how quickly a carefree outing can turn into a time of terror. Many of the ship's young passengers could not swim, and were drowned when the ship struck a rock.

The German passenger liner *Dresden* had a varied career. The ship was built in 1915 and named the *Zeppelin*, but it spent the remainder of World War I laid up. Germany's defeat saw the *Zeppelin* handed over to Britain as part of the war reparations. The vessel was sold on to the Orient Line in 1920, refitted, and renamed the *Ormuz*. Under this name the liner was put to work on the London to Australia route.

The *Ormuz*'s career sailing to Australia ended in April 1927, when an offer for the ship by the North German Lloyd Line was accepted. The liner underwent another refit, was renamed the *Dresden*, and started operating between Bremerhaven and New York. However, part of the *Dresden*'s time was spent as a cruise ship, taking poorer Germans on trips on behalf of the Nazi Party's "Strength Through Joy" campaign.

The *Dresden* was on one such cruise in 1934 when the disaster happened. At about 1930 hours on June 20 the liner struck a submerged rock off Karmoe Island. The impact reverberated around the ship and the passengers, many of whom had never been to sea before and could not swim, began to panic. Some threw themselves into the water. The ship was beached eventually, but with water pouring in through three holes in its hull, there was no chance of it surviving. The *Dresden* began to list and keeled over on to its side the next day. The passengers and crew who survived were taken to several Norwegian coastal towns.

Above: The capsized Dresden. *The ship was taking a party of young Germans on a pleasure cruise when it struck a rock.*

ANDREA DORIA, ATLANTIC

JULY 25, 1956

The *Andrea Doria* was a luxurious, well-appointed liner with modern furnishings that was an immediate hit with its passengers when it began its maiden voyage on January 14, 1953. Its owners, Italia-Sociéta per Azioni di Navigazione, had high hopes for the ship. Yet its life was to end three and a half years later in a shocking collision in thick fog.

The *Andrea Doria* sailed between Genoa and New York, with scheduled stops at Cannes, Naples, and Gibraltar. By the middle of 1956 the *Andrea Doria* had made 50 transatlantic crossings. However, its 51st voyage was to end in catastrophe.

Captain Calamai, the master who had sailed with the *Andrea Doria* on its first voyage, was in command on this trip. As the liner headed out into the Atlantic it had a crew of 572 on board plus 1134 passengers enjoying the ship's facilities, which included three outdoor swimming pools and many public rooms decorated in modern Italian style. The crossing of the Atlantic went without a hitch until the ship was one day out from New York. It was July 25.

The *Andrea Doria* approached Nantucket lightship at full speed but thick fog had reduced visibility to less than half a mile by mid-afternoon. Calamai ordered the liner's speed to be reduced to 21 knots. Shortly after 2230 hours the *Andrea Doria*'s radar operator spotted an object ahead and the ship's officers calculated that the object would pass the liner on its starboard side. Calamai ordered that the ship's fog horn should be sounded every 100 seconds.

Above: The Andrea Doria was a luxury liner plying between Italy and New York.

Calamai ordered his officers to listen out for sounds from the other ship, but they suddenly spotted lights heading directly for them out of the mist. The *Andrea Doria* sent out two warning blasts from its fog horn and attempted to make a sharp turn. However, weighing in at nearly 30,000 gross tons, the *Andrea Doria* was slow to respond to the helm. The second vessel, the Swedish American Line's *Stockholm*, smashed into the *Andrea Doria*'s starboard side.

The damage inflicted was colossal. The *Stockholm* was traveling at 18 knots and had a specially strengthened bow designed to cut through ice. This bow sliced into the *Andrea Doria*'s hull to a depth of 30 feet (9m), the gap running from the liner's upper deck to well below the waterline.

The *Stockholm* was able to reverse engines and pull away from the *Andrea Doria*, which took on an immediate and fatal list. Many of the liner's lifeboats could not be launched because the ship was listing so badly, so the captain delayed broadcasting the order to abandon ship. Instead, he sent out a distress call, which was answered by a number of nearby vessels. These vessels were quickly on the scene and rescued over 1600 of the *Andrea Doria*'s passengers and crew.

The *Stockholm*, although suffering considerable damage to its bow, was also able to aid the rescue effort. When the survivors were counted, it was found that only 47 people had been lost, and most of these had been killed by the initial impact. The *Andrea Doria* sank on July 26, the day after the collision.

Above: *The tangled mass that was the bow of the damaged* Stockholm, *which limped into New York carrying 500 survivors from the* Andrea Doria.

Left: *After the impact with the* Stockholm, *the* Andrea Doria *keeled over to starboard, and the following day sank in 225 feet (68m) of water.*

HANS HEDTOFT, ATLANTIC

JANUARY 30, 1959

The North Atlantic in winter is a treacherous place for shipping. The sea is icy, the weather can be stormy or foggy, and there is the ever-present threat of colliding with an iceberg. Even a ship specially built to withstand these conditions is not immune to disaster, as the fate of the *Hans Hedtoft* shows.

The *Hans Hedtoft* was built for Denmark's Royal Greenland Trading Company to sail between Denmark and Greenland. It was a specific requirement that the ship should provide a year-round service to Greenland, and that the sailings should continue even in the depths of winter, between January and March.

The builders tried to ensure that the vessel could survive the worst the North Atlantic could throw at it by designing the *Hans Hedtoft* with a double bottom, seven watertight compartments, and a reinforced bow. However, even these special features were not enough to protect the ship from the severity of the winter seas in the vicinity of Greenland.

The *Hans Hedtoft* began its maiden voyage on January 7, 1959, sailing out of Copenhagen for Godthaab. On January 29 the ship began the return leg of the voyage, under the command of Captain P. Rasmussen, with 55 passengers and a crew of 40.

On the 30th, the *Hans Hedtoft* faced heavy seas and gale force winds, but was able to make 12 knots. However, the ship collided with an iceberg shortly before 1200 hours some 35 miles (49km) south of Cape Farewell, on the southern tip of Greenland. Rasmussen immediately sent out a distress signal, which was picked up by a US Coast Guard vessel and a trawler.

The trawler raced for the stricken vessel's position but when it arrived it could find nothing. For several days after the loss, ships and aircraft crisscrossed the seas around the *Hans Hedtoft*'s last known position. Visibility was poor and no trace of the vessel could be found. On February 7, the search was called off.

The total loss of the *Hans Hedtoft* on its maiden voyage due to a collision with an iceberg was eerily reminiscent of the loss of the *Titanic*.

Left: The Danish ship Hans Hedtoft *sailing out of Copenhagen on its maiden voyage on January 7, 1959. The ship was destined never to enter Copenhagen harbor again – it sank without trace after colliding with an iceberg on its return voyage.*

CARIBIA, GUAM
AUGUST 13, 1974

Dogged by misfortune throughout its life, the passenger liner *Caribia* had an ignominious end when it was smashed to pieces on its way to the scrap yard.

The *Caribia* was not the most fortunate of ships. It was launched as the *Caronia* in late October 1947 and began its working life on the Southampton to New York line. However, the growing competition from air travel was making things hard for the Atlantic passenger liners, and the *Caronia* was far from profitable. Although the ship was popular as a Caribbean cruiser, in 1967 the owners, Cunard, bowed to the inevitable and the *Caronia* was withdrawn from service.

The *Caronia* was sold in 1968 and was renamed the *Caribia*. After a refit in Piraeus its new owners decided to try their luck in the cruise market out of New York. But the change of name did not seem to improve the ship's fortunes. After the *Caribia* set out on its second cruise on February 28, 1969, a steam line in the boiler room exploded on March 5, killing a crew member. The ship lost power and was eventually towed back to New York and sold.

The *Caribia* had problems finding a permanent berth in New York. It finally fell foul of the harbor authorities and was fined for "parking" illegally! The difficulties of finding a berth were settled at the beginning of 1971 and the *Caribia* docked at Pier 56. The vessel was, however, a huge drain on the owner's financial resources and a way to dispose of it was sought. Because the *Caribia* was no longer considered a viable business, its owner finally accepted an offer from a Taiwanese scrap yard.

On January 25, 1974, the ship sailed from New York on its final journey. It was towed by the tug *Hamburg*. Bad weather forced the tug and its charge to put into Guam, but as the two entered harbor on August 13, the *Caribia* smashed into a breakwater. The ship capsized and broke into three sections. The remains were later broken up in situ.

Above: The Cunard liner Caribia *was built for the transatlantic route, but by the time the ship started sailing the route, air travel was making the passenger liners unnecessary.*

ATLANTIC EMPRESS, CARIBBEAN

JULY 19, 1979

The loss of the 292,666-ton *Atlantic Empress* supertanker was the result of a collision with another monster supertanker, the 210,257-ton *Aegean Captain*. Both tankers were Liberian registered. The *Aegean Captain* had recently filled up with crude oil in Venezuela and was bound for Singapore, while the *Atlantic Empress* was making its way from Beaumont, Texas, to the Persian Gulf. The combined loss of crude oil into the Caribbean was estimated at about 280,000 tons. Lloyd's of London, the maritime insurers, described the disaster as "our biggest marine loss".

The collision occurred a little way off the island of Little Tobago in the early evening at a time when the weather was worsening. As night fell visibility in the area began to drop quickly, yet although both ships had modern radar systems, no one on watch on either ship appears to have spotted that the two supertankers were closing fast. It was not until the two ships were about one mile apart that lookouts spotted the danger. By then, however, it was far to late to do anything. Supertankers take a long time to stop or maneuver and neither option was available at such a short distance. The tankers struck each other with a combined speed of 30 knots.

It was just after 1900 hours when the *Aegean Captain*'s bow crashed into the *Atlantic Empress*'s port side. Fires were ignited on both vessels. The crew of the *Aegean Captain* were able to make an orderly evacuation of their vessel, but things did not go so smoothly on the *Atlantic Empress*. The crew had difficulty launching their lifeboats and of the 42 people on board the tanker 26 died. The *Aegean Captain* was towed back to Curacao in the Dutch Antilles but the *Atlantic Empress* sank.

Below: Clouds of dense smoke billow from the doomed Atlantic Empress *after its collision with another super tanker, the* Aegean Captain.

DONA PAZ, PHILIPPINES

DECEMBER 20, 1987

The treacherous waters dividing the many islands that make up the Philippines have been the scene of many shipwrecks, but the incident involving the *Doña Paz*, a workhorse ferry used on the inter-island routes, ranks as one of the most horrific disasters ever to befall any vessel.

The *Doña Paz*'s last voyage took place at one of the busiest times of the year, when demand on the Philippine ferries is at its highest. The ferry was operating on the Leyte-Manila route and sailed from Tacloban for the capital packed with locals anxious to finish their preparations for the Christmas festival. There were so many passengers crowded on to the *Doña Paz* that many went unrecorded, so the lists of casualties after the disaster were far from accurate.

The first leg of the voyage was completed without any problems being encountered but disaster struck as the *Doña Paz* entered on the last third of its scheduled run and was just off the small island of Marinduque.

It was a dark, moonless night and many of the passsengers were sleeping on deck as best they could under the crowded conditions. Without any warning, the ferry suddenly collided with a tanker, the *Victor*. The impact was followed almost immediately by fire and the *Doña Paz* was quickly engulfed and sank. The surrounding sea was covered with blazing oil from the tanker and people in the water had little chance of survival. The few who did manage to escape the flames had to spend most of the night clinging to wreckage as the rescue effort did not get under way until daylight. Even then, the weather conspired to make rescue difficult. Heavy thunderstorms blanketed the area.

When the investigation was completed, it was estimated that the two vessels together were carrying 1556 passengers and crew, but this was almost certainly an underestimate. The figure was probably much higher. Only 30 people survived the collision and subsequent flames, and many of the bodies were never recovered from the sea.

Above: The inter-island ferry, the Doña Paz, *on one of its regular voyages.*

FIRE

Many vessels have succumbed to the dangers of fire. In the age of wooden ships this was hardly surprising but even modern ships built from metal face the same danger. Cargo ships often carry highly combustible materials in their holds, while passenger ships may be fitted out with highly flammable furnishings. And even metals such as aluminum will burn at high temperatures.

The ship's captain has several responsibilities in the event of a fire. He must alert any passengers on board, prepare to put evacuation procedures in train, fight the fire, and if the situation cannot quickly be brought under control, send out a distress call. In most of the shipwrecks described in this chapter one or several of these procedures have not been carried out. The most remarkable example is perhaps that of the *Yarmouth Castle*, a ship that was engulfed by flames in 1965. The captain was not informed for some time, and even when he was informed he considered the fire manageable, and did not give the order to abandon ship until the vessel was clearly beyond saving. He was also unable to send out a distress call because the radio room was in flames. In contravention of normal maritime procedure, he and his crew were among the first to abandon ship.

The *Yarmouth Castle* incident is, thankfully, comparatively rare. Crews have become highly proficient at dealing with fires and ships now have extremely efficient fire-control systems. Perhaps what is most important is speed of response and judgment. It is crucial that the potential dangers are assessed quickly and accurately and that the required procedures are put in operation. However, as the following examples show, even the most prompt response is not always sufficient to save a vessel from destruction.

Right: The Italian liner Achille Lauro *on fire and adrift in the sea off the Somali coast the day after 1000 passengers and crew were rescued from the ship's lifeboats.*

SAALE, NEW YORK

JUNE 30, 1900

Harbors are meant to be places of safety and refuge for ships but, as the fate of the *Saale* shows, this is not always the case. This liner caught fire from a conflagration on the pier while the ship was "safely" berthed.

The two-funneled *Saale* was owned by the North German Lloyd line and its home port was Bremen. The ship had accommodation to cater for over 1200 passengers, of whom 150 could enjoy the privilege of first class travel. The *Saale* worked between Bremen, Southampton, and New York.

In late June 1900, the *Saale* was docked at Hoboken, New Jersey, in the company of three other North German Lloyd ships – the *Bremen*, the *Kaiser Wilhelm der Grosse*, and the *Main*. A fire started on the adjacent pier three among a pile of cotton bales and spread to barrels of oil and turpentine stored nearby. Strong winds assisted the spread of the fire and the

docked ships were in danger of being consumed. The *Kaiser Wilhelm* made steam and edged away from the growing conflagration but the other ships caught fire.

Those on the upper deck of the *Saale* were able to escape by leaping into the Hudson River. Unfortunately those below deck were trapped. Some tried to escape through the portholes but these proved to be too small for anyone to get through. The burnt-out *Saale* settled on the bottom of the dock.

When the wreck was investigated, it was found that the carnage below decks was horrific. The charred remains of 99 passengers and crew were brought out. One positive result of the disaster was that ships in the future were built with portholes big enough to escape through in an emergency.

The *Saale* was repaired and continued to have an active life for 24 more years, though not as a passenger ship. In 1924 the *Saale*, renamed the *Madison*, was scrapped in Italy.

Below: The German liner the Saale, *which was berthed in Hoboken, New Jersey, when a fire on the adjacent pier spread to the ship, with horrific results.*

CITY OF HONOLULU, PACIFIC

OCTOBER 12, 1922

When fire breaks out on a ship at sea it can be a terrifying experience. Fire can quickly take over and engulf even the largest of ships, as the fate of the *City of Honolulu* illustrates.

The *City of Honolulu* began life as the *Friedrich der Grosse*, part of the fleet owned by North German Lloyd. The *Friedrich* was used until the outbreak of World War I on the route between Australia and the North Atlantic. However, North German Lloyd lost the ship at the beginning of World War I when, in August 1914, the first month of the war, it was interned in New York harbor.

By 1917, the year the United States entered the war, the US Navy needed to build up its transport fleet to ferry scores of thousands of troops to the Western Front. The *Friedrich der Grosse* fitted the bill, was renamed the *Huron*, and converted to use as a troopship. As the *Huron*, the vessel survived the war and in 1922 was chartered out to the Los Angeles Steamship Company. Renamed (yet again) the *City of Honolulu*, the liner began sailing between California and the Hawaiian Islands in September 1922.

The *City of Honolulu* never completed its maiden voyage. Returning to California, fire broke out some 650 miles (1040km) out from San Pedro on October 12. The fire quickly took over the ship, which was completedly gutted. A distress call quickly brought the freighter *West Faralon* to the scene, and all of the 70 passengers and 145 crew on board the *City of Honolulu* were rescued .

The burnt-out and abandoned *City of Honolulu* drifted for five days before being sunk by gunfire from, ironically, a US Navy warship, the *Thomas*.

Right: To prevent a panic when fire broke out, the captain of the City of Honolulu *ordered the band to play so that passengers could dance until the lifeboats were ready.*

GEORGES PHILIPPAR, GULF OF ADEN

MAY 15, 1932

The French passenger liner *Georges Philippar* was no stranger to fire. The ship it was built to replace, the *Paul Lacat*, was burnt out in Marseille harbor in December 1928 and the *Georges Philippar* itself was ravaged by fire on November 29, 1930, some three weeks before its launch. The interior was badly damaged but fortunately its luxurious fittings were yet to be added. The ship was finally completed in January 1932.

The ship's first and last voyage began under a cloud – French police warned the *Georges Philippar*'s owners, Messageries Maritimes, that threats had been made to destroy the vessel on February 26. The outward journey to Yokohama passed without incident. The ship made a quick turnaround and headed for home, calling first at Shanghai and then Colombo. From Colombo the vessel headed across the Indian Ocean, carrying 518 passengers and 347 crew members. Twice during this leg a fire alarm went off in a store room containing a large quantity of bullion. On both occasions no fire was found.

A fire did break out early in the morning of May 15 in a cabin. The danger was only belatedly reported to the master, Captain Vieg, and by this time the fire had spread. The captain decided to head for Aden at speed and beach the vessel, but unfortunately the high speed only served to fan the flames.

Vieg realized that the fire was out of control and opted to abandon ship. Three vessels answered the *Georges Philippar*'s distress call and rescued over 650 of those on board. Estimates of the fatalities varied between 40 and 90. The *Georges Philippar* burned and drifted for four days before sinking on May 19.

Below: The French liner Georges Philippar was an attractive-looking ship. But its maiden voyage to Yokohama and back was never completed – the ship succumbed to fire in the Gulf of Aden and sank.

PIETER CORNELISZOON HOOFT, AMSTERDAM

NOVEMBER 14, 1932

The life of the Dutch liner *Pieter Corneliszoon Hooft* was destined to begin and end with fire. Commissioned by the Nederland Line from a French shipyard, the ship had its first brush with disaster on December 25, 1925, while it was still in the shipyard. The vessel was engulfed by a major fire that left its passenger accommodation in ruins. The French builders could not meet the deadline for finishing construction, so the ship was sent to Amsterdam for completion.

Amsterdam was to prove a fatal home for the *Pieter Corneliszoon Hooft*. The ship was eventually completed and delivered to its owners in August 1926. Its maiden voyage, from Amsterdam to the Dutch East Indies, was made the same year. It was a money-spinning route and the Nederland Line decided to improve the *Pieter Corneliszoon Hooft*'s performance. In 1930, the ship was lengthened by nine feet (3m) and was fitted with new diesel engines. Its first voyage after the refit took place in April 1931.

The ship did not survive for long after its refit. On November 14, 1932, the liner was engulfed by fire while docked at Amsterdam's Sumatra Quay. The local emergency services reacted quickly to prevent damage to the harbor, using tugs to tow the *Pieter Corneliszoon Hooft* to safe water, but the fire was out of control and the Amsterdam fire services were unable to save the liner. The vessel was left far beyond repair by the inferno and had to be sold for scrap.

Above: When the Pieter Corneliszoon Hooft caught fire while berthed in Amsterdam harbor, tugs were quickly mobilized to tow the burning ship away from the docks.

L'ATLANTIQUE, ENGLISH CHANNEL

JANUARY 4, 1933

The Companie de Navigation Sud Atlantique was justifiably proud of the 42,512-gross ton *L'Atlantique* – it was the largest and most luxurious passenger ship plying the route to South America. The *L'Atlantique* was launched in 1931 and made its maiden voyage, between Bordeaux and Buenos Aires, on September 29, 1931. The disaster that befell the *L'Atlantique* 15 months later, however, led to a bitter law case and the vessel never put to sea again.

The fateful incident took place as the *L'Atlantique* was heading from its home port of Bordeaux to Le Havre for its regular yearly spell in drydock for maintenance. At about 0330 hours the ship's master, Captain Schoofs, was informed that a fire had broken out on E Deck in cabin 232. The fire spread rapidly and the crew was forced to abandon ship. In the confusion 17 lives were lost. The blaze continued for two days. The *L'Atlantique* drifted toward the coast of southwest England before it was taken in tow by tugs from France, Germany, and the Netherlands on January 6. It was docked at Cherbourg.

When the damage was assessed, the owners claimed the ship was a write-off and put in a claim for its full insured value. The insurers, however, disagreed, estimating that the vessel could be repaired for considerably less. The owners won the subsequent legal battle, and the *L'Atlantique* never sailed again. In 1936 it was sold for its scrap value.

Below: The French liner L'Atlantique *ablaze in the English Channel in January 1933. The ship was eventually taken in tow to Cherbourg.*

PARIS, LE HAVRE

APRIL 19, 1939

The owners of the *Paris*, the Companie Générale Transatlantique, wanted to build a palace of the high seas to cash in on the highly profitable transatlantic passenger service. Its first-class passenger rooms were sumptuously decorated in the art nouveau style, and the whole ship was designed to give passengers the feeling that they were already in France.

Below: After being ravaged by fire all night, the French liner Paris *sinks in the dock at Le Havre.*

Work began on the liner shortly before World War I. Construction of the *Paris* was started by Chantiers et Ateliers de St Nazaire in 1913, but when war broke out work was stopped in 1914. With slipway space in high demand, the building was subsequently resumed and

the *Paris* was launched in mid-September 1916. When the fitting-out work was completed in June 1921 the *Paris* was, at 34,569 gross tons, the largest passenger ship ever built by French yards. Its owners had also ensured that its more than 550 first class passengers would enjoy luxurious surroundings and almost unparalleled on-board facilities. The *Paris* made its first transatlantic trip from Le Havre via Plymouth to New York on June 15, 1921.

The first disaster to strike the *Paris* occurred in August 1929 while the vessel was docked at Le Havre. A fire broke out, which destroyed a large part of the ship's passenger accommodation. It is possible that the fire was due to arson, since the shipping company had

received a warning that its ships might be sabotaged. Faced with an extensive refit, the company decided to revamp and improve the ship's accommodation. By January 1930 the refitting had been completed and the *Paris* was put back into service.

World War II was just a few months away when fire struck the *Paris* for the second time. The ship was again docked at Le Havre. On April 19, 1939, several fires broke out at the same time – one began in the vessel's bakery and two others started on two of its upper decks. Despite the fact that the ship was in harbor, the emergency services were unable to prevent the fires from spreading and the blaze was soon out of

control. Eventually the *Paris* capsized and sank at the dockside. Only part of its hull and superstructure remained visible above the harbor's waters. Again there were rumors that the *Paris* had been the victim of a deliberate act of arson.

World War II prevented the ship being raised. The last chapter in the sorry saga of the *Paris* began shortly after the end of the war. In 1946 another ship, the *Liberté*, broke free from its moorings and crashed into the remains of the *Paris*. It was the final blow. The *Liberté* was towed free, but the *Paris* was clearly beyond hope of salvation. In 1947 any plans to raise the liner were abandoned and the ship was scrapped.

Right: The Paris *lies on its side in the dock, where it was to remain for eight years before it was finally scrapped.*

LAKONIA, ATLANTIC

DECEMBER 22, 1963

For some of the 651 passengers and 385 crew who embarked for a Christmas cruise aboard the Greek Line's 20,314 gross ton *Lakonia* on December 19, 1963, the voyage was to be the most memorable of their lives. But for more than 130 of them, it was destined to be their last voyage. The *Lakonia* set sail from Southampton on the south coast of England at the start of an 11-day cruise to the Canary Islands.

The *Lakonia* was not a new ship. It had been completed by Nederlandsche Shipbuilding in 1931 for the Nederland Royal Mail Line. The company intended that their new liner, called the *Johan van Oldenbarnevelt*, should serve the Dutch East Indies from Amsterdam. World War II intervened and the ship served as a troop transport, but returned to its old route in 1946. It later sailed to Australia packed with migrants, underwent a number of refits, and then trans-

ferred to the lucrative round-the-world cruise business. In 1962 it was sold to the Greek Line, renamed the *Lakonia*, and began serving the Southampton-Canary Islands route in spring 1963.

The Christmas cruise began to go wrong on December 22 when the *Lakonia* was some 180 miles (288km) north of the island of Madeira. A fire started in the ship's hairdressing salon. A large bang followed, possibly caused by pressurized containers in the salon exploding, and thick black smoke began to spread throughout the vessel. In the confusion many passengers began to panic.

The ship's crew, operating under the command of Captain M. Zarbis, gave orders that life-preservers should be put on, but that was as far as the emergency instructions went. There seems to have been a problem with the ship's public address system. Instructions given by word of mouth to passengers were conflicting. Some were told to stay below in their cabins,

Above: Smoke pours from the stricken liner Lakonia *as it is engulfed by fire about 180 miles (288km) north of Madeira.*

Right: Even though the Norwegian tug Herkules *attempted to tow the burning* Lakonia *to port, the liner was too badly damaged to save, and sank soon after this picture was taken.*

Right: Even though the Norwegian tug Herkules *attempted to tow the burning* Lakonia *to port, the liner was too badly damaged to save, and sank soon after this picture was taken.*

Right: An injured passenger from the Lakonia *is lifted on board one of the rescue ships after being picked up by one of the lifeboats.*

others to go to the dining room. Passengers who managed to climb up to the boat deck found a scene of confusion – the crew seemed to be having considerable difficulty in launching the available lifeboats.

The *Lakonia* was able to send out a distress call that was heeded by a number of vessels sailing in the vicinity. The first to arrive was the *Salta*, an Argentinian passenger liner. The *Salta* was joined by four other vessels – the *Centaur, Charlesville, Export Aide,* and *Montcalm.* Working in unison, the rescuers took on board over 900 people from the *Lakonia.* Nearly 90 people were known to have died in the fire and a further 42 were unaccounted for but presumed dead.

The *Lakonia* itself was too far gone to save. The fire had taken an irreversible hold on the ship. A Norwegian salvage tug, the *Herkules,* was able to get a line out to the *Lakonia* on Christmas Eve and began to head for the nearest port. However, the damage to the *Lakonia* was far too great for it to stay afloat and the liner succumbed to the Atlantic on December 29.

YARMOUTH CASTLE, CARIBBEAN

NOVEMBER 13, 1965

The *Yarmouth Castle* had a long, if not particularly distinguished, career. Launched in 1927 as the *Evangeline*, the liner served with the US Navy during World War II. It was bought by its final owners, Yarmouth Cruise Lines, in 1963. The owners renamed the ship, but the new name could not revitalize the aging vessel, which was plagued by engine problems. Yarmouth Lines decided to switch the vessel to the cruise route from Miami to Nassau in the Bahamas.

In November 1965, the *Yarmouth Castle*, with 372 passengers and 174 crew members on board, set sail for Nassau. At around 0035 hours on the night of November 13 a fire broke out in cabin 610 and quickly spread along the ship's corridors to the decks above. The ship's master, Captain Byron Voutsinas, was not told of the fire for 25 minutes. He investigated the blaze and returned to the bridge, but failed to send out a distress signal. In fact, the fire was so out of control that he had to give the signal to abandon ship some 20 minutes later. By this time the flames had engulfed the bridge, and a large number of lifeboats. The ship's radio room was also ablaze, so that distress signals could not be sent out.

Two ships, the *Finnpulp* and the *Bahama Star*, did spot the burning *Yarmouth Castle* and raced to its aid. The first lifeboat to be picked up included Captain Voutsinas and some of his officers. Many of the ship's passengers had to be rescued from the sea. The two rescue ships eventually saved over 450 passengers and crew, but there was no saving the *Yarmouth Castle*. The ship, ablaze from bow to stern, heeled over in the early morning and sank.

Above: This dramatic picture of the Yarmouth Castle *ablaze was taken by a passenger on the* Bahama Star, *one of the ships that went to the rescue. An unlaunched lifeboat can be seen on the left.*

SEAWISE UNIVERSITY, HONG KONG

JANUARY 9, 1972

Despite its unfamiliar name, the *Seawise University* was in fact one of the most famous vessels of the 20th century. The largest passenger liner ever built, the *Queen Elizabeth* (as the ship was called for most of its life), was launched shortly before World War II. In fact, war broke out before the ship was completed. The *Queen Elizabeth* spent most of the war dodging German submarines and made a significant contribution to the Allied military effort. It transported over 800,000 soldiers between 1940 and 1946.

After the war the *Queen Elizabeth* was refitted to carry out its intended task – fast, luxurious travel across the Atlantic between England and New York. The *Queen Elizabeth*, along with the *Queen Mary*, which had also had a distinguished wartime career, enjoyed a brief moment in the limelight, but the truth of the matter was that the age of luxury sea travel was drawing to a close. Despite expensive refits and ever more opulent furnishings, the great liner was losing out to air travel. The *Queen Elizabeth* was sold to the United States but plans to turn it into a tourist attraction never reached fruition. In 1970 the liner, anchored at Florida's Port Everglades, was sold to C.Y. Tung.

C.Y. Tung had grand plans for the *Queen Elizabeth*. The ship was renamed and was to sail to Hong Kong where, at enormous cost, it would be transformed into a floating university. It was also envisaged that the ship would be used for cruises. Because of problems with the aging ship's boilers, the *Seawise University* took six months to sail from Port Everglades to Hong Kong, where it arrived in July 1971.

Neither of the new owner's schemes was ever achieved. While the extensive refit was being carried out in Hong Kong harbor, the ship was sabotaged. On January 9, 1972, it seems that several fires erupted simultaneously in different locations throughout the ship. The blaze was finally reported to the harbor authorities at 1030 hours by a helicopter flying over the

Left: The Queen Elizabeth *was the world's largest passenger liner, and the pride of its owner, the Cunard Line.*

Above: Fireboats battle with the flames as Seawise University *(the former* Queen Elizabeth) *burns in Hong Kong harbor.*

ship. The ship's own fire-fighting system proved inadequate to deal with the flames, which spread rapidly through five of the ship's 11 decks. The explosion of an oil tank then added to the conflagration. Those working on the vessel could do nothing more than flee for their lives.

When the Hong Kong firefighting services arrived to deal with the fire, they faced a virtually impossible task – most of the *Seawise University*'s superstructure was ablaze and, as the hours passed, the liner began to list dangerously. The main centers of fire were finally extinguished at daybreak on January 10, but by this time the ship was too badly damaged to stay afloat. The once-great liner rolled over on its side, coming to rest in 40 feet (12m) of water. Dismantling of the vessel got underway in 1974.

Right: Despite the efforts of the firefighters, the liner keeled over, coming to rest on the seabed of the harbor.

LEONARDO DA VINCI, LA SPEZIA

JULY 3, 1980

The 33,340-gross ton *Leonardo da Vinci* was an elegant and luxurious liner that was built to replace the ill-fated *Andrea Doria*, which went to the bottom in 1956 following a collision with another vessel. The *Leonardo da Vinci* was built by Ansaldo SpA of Genoa and was launched in early December 1958.

The vessel was opulently fitted out – it had five swimming pools and 30 public rooms designed in modern Italian style – and it was an immediate hit with passengers when it began sailing between Genoa and New York. As well as plying the transatlantic route, the *Leonardo da Vinci* also sailed as a cruise ship in many

of the world's oceans. In July 1977 the ship was transferred to Italian Line Cruises International to be used for short cruises between Florida's Port Everglades and Nassau in the Bahamas, but the scheme was far from successful. The *Leonardo da Vinci* was returned to La Spezia, laid up, and offered for sale in 1978.

The liner never sailed again. On July 3, 1980, a fire broke out in the ship's chapel and engulfed the whole vessel. The La Spezia fire service was unable to bring the fire under control and the *Leonardo da Vinci* was towed out of the harbor to burn itself out. The ship eventually heeled over and capsized. The *Leonardo* was raised in March 1981 but was too badly damaged for repair and was scrapped the following year.

Below: After being consumed by flames for three days, the burned-out hulk of the Leonardo da Vinci *lies on its side in La Spezia harbor.*

PRINSENDAM, PACIFIC

OCTOBER 4, 1980

Above: *A US Coast Guard helicopter hovers over the crippled* Prinsendam *as it is towed through the waters of the Gulf of Alaska.*

Right: *A lifeboat full of survivors from the burning* Prinsendam. *All on board were rescued safely and taken to coastal settlements in Alaska.*

The fate of the *Prinsendam* shows how the total loss of a ship need not be accompanied by loss of life. When fire broke out on the vessel the captain and crew followed the correct procedures, with the result that all the passengers and crew were evacuated and saved.

Built by Rotterdam's De Merwede Shipyards in 1972, the *Prinsendam*'s career as a cruise liner lasted only until 1980. A forewarning of its eventual fate came in April 1973 when a fire destroyed the ship's passenger accommodation and much of its superstructure.

When repairs had been completed, the *Prinsendam* was sent out to the Far East. The intention was for the ship to cruise around Indonesia, but the business was far from profitable and the ship was switched to the Vancouver and Singapore cruise trade.

The ship sailed from Vancouver during the winter, but switched to Singapore during the summer. In late 1980 the *Prinsendam* was based at Vancouver. In early October the vessel took on board over 300 passengers

Below: The scene on board the Prinsendam *after the passengers had been safely evacuated. Charred and blistered paintwork is evidence of the intense heat of the fire that had raged through the early hours of the morning.*

for a 29-day cruise. Soon after midnight on October 4, as the *Prinsendam* made its way through the Gulf of Alaska, a fire started in one of its main engines. The crew acted quickly, sealing off the area, and dowsing the flames with carbon dioxide, which should have extinguished the flames. However, when they moved back into the area of the fire, it rapidly became clear that the flames were still spreading.

Recognizing the severity of the situation, the captain sent out a distress call shortly after 0100 hours. The response was swift – helicopters, the US Coast Guard, and the supertanker *Williamsburgh* hastened to the stricken ship. Meanwhile the *Prinsendam*'s crew redoubled their efforts to halt the spread of the flames. It was to no avail. The fire led to a failure in the ship's electrical circuits, and water pressure, essential to the firefighters' efforts, plummeted. The ship's master, Captain Cornelius Wabeke, had no other option. At 0515 hours he gave the order to abandon ship.

The evacuation proceeded without panic and the passengers made their way safely into the lifeboats. The captain and 50 volunteers elected to stay on board to fight the fire but little could be done. By mid-afternoon, the situation was beyond saving and Wabeke and his team also abandoned ship. All the passengers and crew were picked up by the rescue vessels and landed at a number of coastal settlements in Alaska.

The ship was now empty and was drifting. On October 7 a tug, the *Commodore Straits*, attempted to tow the *Prinsendam* back to Portland. The tug was able to get a line on the *Prinsendam* but the weather was worsening. The vessel was slowly but surely listing and taking on water from the rough seas. The fires on deck burned themselves out on October 10 but those below raged unabated. The ship's list was also worsening and on the morning of October 11, it was clear it could not survive. The *Commodore Straits* cut its line and the *Prinsendam* sank at 0835 hours

REINA DEL MAR, MEDITERRANEAN

MAY 28, 1981

The *Reina del Mar* began life in 1951 as the *Ocean Monarch*, and served with a number of passenger lines, changing its name in 1967 to the *Varna*, before being sold to a Greek shipping line in 1978. But the ship was destroyed by fire before it ever put to sea for its final owners.

The ship that was first called the *Ocean Monarch* was built in 1951 by a British shipyard, Vickers Armstrong, to serve the route between New York and Bermuda for Furness Withy. As the *Varna*, it was next owned by a Bulgarian company that chartered it out as a cruise ship sailing out of Montreal in the early 1970s. It then had a brief career with Sovereign Cruises from 1973.

The *Varna* made just two cruises for Sovereign and was laid up until 1978, when it was bought by a Greek shipping line based in Pireaus. The new owners decided to change the ship's name to *Rivera*. The company had big plans to use the *Rivera* as a cruise ship, but they were slow in getting off the ground. In 1981 the *Rivera* was renamed *Reina del Mar*, and this seemed to do the trick. The owners announced that the *Reina del Mar* would commence a series of Mediterranean cruises in 1981.

But first it was decided to renovate the vessel. During the work a fire broke out on May 28 in the ship's boiler room and quickly spread through the vessel, devastating the passenger accommodation. The ship was left in a dangerous condition – it was burnt out and its superstructure had collapsed. As it was a hazard to other ships, the *Reina del Mar* was towed to safety close to the *Rasa Sayang*, another burnt-out vessel. However, the *Reina del Mar* capsized and went to the bottom off the yard at Perama on May 31.

Above: The Reina del Mar *berthed at Southampton in May 1974, seven years before the fatal fire that sent it to the bottom.*

LAVIA, HONG KONG

JANUARY 7, 1989

The process of refitting can be a dangerous operation for a ship, it seems. As with the *Reina del Mar*, the fire that ended the life of the *Lavia* broke out while the vessel was in harbor undergoing a refit programme.

The *Lavia* (first called the *Media*) was built in 1947 by John Brown and Company of Glasgow for the Cunard Line. Fitted with twin-screws and steam turbines, the *Media* was the first new passenger ship to be built for the transatlantic route since the end of World War II. Cunard had initially intended the vessel to be a cargo-carrier but had a change of heart. The *Media* was refitted with cabins to carry 250 first class passengers.

By August 1947 the *Media* was ready to ply the seas between Liverpool and New York. However, the advent of fast jet travel between Europe and North America in the late 1950s was to put an end to the era of the great transatlantic liners. The *Media* was also too slow to compete with the new cargo-carriers being brought into service. Its career now began a downward spiral that would end in disaster.

In the early 1960s the *Media* was sold to the Italian Codegar Line and refitted in Genoa to carry 1320 passengers in tourist class. Renamed the *Flavia*, the vessel served the booming round-the-world cruise market and the lucrative trade transporting emigrants to Australia, but this upturn in its fortunes did not last.

Below: The large quantities of water used to put out the fire on the Lavia caused it to capsize. It was later sold for scrap.

Above: *The* Lavia *smoldering in Hong Kong harbor, with a fireboat alongside.*

After the Codegar Line was taken over by the Costa Line in 1968, the *Flavia* cruised between Miami and various Caribbean islands until 1982. After nearly 35 years in service around the world, the *Flavia* was showing its age and its turbines were becoming less and less efficient. A Chinese business based in Hong Kong, the Virtue Shipping Company, took on the *Flavia*, intending to convert it into a casino cruise ship. The ship was renamed the *Flavian* but did not prove popular and remained for most of the time at its moorings in Hong Kong harbor.

Perhaps hoping for a change of fortune, the Virtue Shipping Company changed the ship's name yet again,

to the *Lavia*, in 1986, and decided to have the vessel refitted. The refitting work began but was never completed. In January 1989 a fire used by workmen got out of control and the flames spread through the ship's cabins. As the *Lavia* was in harbor, emergency vessels were soon on the scene. Four Hong Kong fireboats and more than 250 firemen attacked the flames, but the ship was fatally damaged, and the vast quantities of water that were sprayed over the fire caused the ship to heel over and capsize.

None of the 35 workers or nine crew on the vessel was injured, but the *Lavia*'s days were over. The ship was refloated, towed to Taiwan and scrapped.

SCANDINAVIAN STAR, BALTIC SEA

APRIL 7, 1990

t is rare for a ship to be the target of an arsonist. However, the *Scandinavian Star*, a 10,513-ton ferry capable of carrying up to 810 passengers, was wrecked by a deliberately started fire. This horrifying incident made headline news around the world, and led to the tightening up of international security and safety regulations for passenger ships.

The *Scandinavian Star* (which had several other former names) was built in Nantes, France, in 1971 and was used on a number of routes before being chartered by the Danish Da-No Line. The *Scandinavian Star* operated between Frederikshaven and Oslo.

Passengers on board at the time of the incident reported that the arsonist had struck twice. The first blaze had been spotted and extinguished. The second, however, spread rapidly and was soon out of control. Four other ferries and a number of cargo ships went to the aid of the imperilled *Star* and rescued many of the passengers and crew. Initial reports indicated that

there were no fatalities, but this was not the case. Investigators discovered that at least 150 passengers and crew had died, but the figure was probably higher.

Tthe total number of passengers aboard the *Star* will never be known as the relevant papers were destroyed in the fire and many children were probably not recorded on them anyway. The disaster raised many questions over the ferry's safety procedures: some lifeboats could not be launched and the sprinkler systems were ineffective. Because there were so many different nationalities on board – among both passengers and crew – there were communication difficulties, and in the resulting confusion people panicked and fought to get off the ship.

The fire finally burned out after four days and the still-smoldering *Star* was towed into Lysekil.The *Star* eventually made its way to Southampton and was sold to International Shipping partners in early 1994. Renamed the *Regal Voyager*, the ship was subsequently converted in Italy to carry cargo.

Below: The still-smoldering ferry, the Scandinavian Star, *in the small Swedish harbor of Lysekil, where it was towed after the disaster.*

ACHILLE LAURO, INDIAN OCEAN

NOVEMBER 30, 1994

Left: The Italian liner Achille Lauro *on fire 100 miles (160km) off the coast of Somalia.*

I f a ship can be said to be lucky or unlucky then the *Achille Lauro* must rank as one of the unluckiest. Before being sent to the bottom by fire in 1994, the vessel had already been plagued by misfortune. In 1971 the *Achille Lauro* rammed an Italian fishing boat, leaving one of its crew dead; in 1981 two passengers died while trying to escape a fire on board the vessel; and in 1985 the ship was hijacked by Palestinians and one of its passengers, an invalid, was murdered.

The 23,629-gross ton *Achille Lauro* took nearly 10 years to build. No sooner had it been laid down for the Royal Rotterdam Lloyd line than construction was halted by World War II. It was finally completed in 1947. The *Achille Lauro*, originally known as the *Willem Ruys*, plied the route between the Netherlands and East Indies until it transferred to sailing around the world in 1959. In the mid-1960s the ship carried migrants from Europe to Australia, but was finally bought by StarLauro of Naples for full-time cruising.

On November 30, 1994, the *Achille Lauro* was cruising off the Horn of Africa with 1000 passengers on board. A fire broke out and spread fast, forcing passengers and crew to take to the lifeboats.

The ship began to list to port as the fire continued to blaze for 48 hours. The end came as a tug was attempting to get a line on board. The ship was rocked by explosion and went to the bottom. There were reports of two casualties. Remarkably, two of the *Achille Lauro*'s sister ships – the *Lakonia* and the *Angelina Lauro* – also succumbed to fire.

Left: Survivors *from the* Achille Lauro *disembark from the US cruiser* Gettysburg *at Djibouti.*

EXPLOSION

This chapter looks at a number of incidents in which an explosion has sent a ship to the bottom. A few of the events related here involve some military action, but these do not include out-and-out warships sunk by enemy action. So the controversial sinking of the *Lusitania* in 1915 is included, although there remains much debate as to the liner's true role in World War I.

Most of the explosions described here have, however, occurred during wartime or shortly before the outbreak of war. The loss of the battleship USS *Maine* was, in fact, used as a pretext by the United States to go to war with Spain in 1898. Most of the other vessels to be lost to explosion during a period of hostilities have been victims of either mines or, more commonly, torpedoes. Others have been destroyed in part due to the cargoes they were carrying at the time of the incident.

The worst example of this was the *Mont Blanc*, which was packed with TNT. In 1917, a collision led to the detonation of the cargo, which obliterated a large part of the Canadian port of Halifax. A similar event, although in peacetime, left much of Texas City in ruins in 1947. Clearly more ships carry dangerous cargoes in wartime but dangerous situations of this kind can also occur in times of peace.

There are stringent safeguards and regulations that govern the transport of dangerous chemicals and the like. These are of no avail during wartime, but in times of peace no one in charge of cargo vessels can afford to ignore or flout them. Accidents do happen leading to explosions at sea, and only constant vigilance will keep them to a minimum.

Right: The USS Maine, *which was anchored in Havana harbor, Cuba, when it was destroyed by an explosion in February 1898. The incident led to the United States declaring war on Spain.*

USS MAINE, HAVANA

FEBRUARY 15, 1898

No one knows exactly what caused the explosion that led to the sinking of the 6682-ton battleship USS *Maine*, but there have been a number of theories, some more probable than others. What is certain is that the sinking of the warship on February 15, 1898, resulted in the deaths of 258 enlisted men and three officers. It was the worst loss of life suffered in peacetime by the US Navy up to that date, and it led to the United States declaring war on Spain in April 1898.

The *Maine* was anchored in Havana harbor, Cuba (which was a Spanish colony at the time) to protect US citizens on that increasingly volatile island and to evacuate them if the fighting between the Cuban insurgents and the Spanish authorities took a turn for the worse. The United States had expressed support for the insurgents, but there were no hostilities between the United States and Spain when the *Maine* sailed into Havana on January 25.

Both sides observed the usual diplomatic formalities, the US ship exchanging salutes with the Spanish warships at anchor. The *Maine*'s commander, Captain Charles Sigsbee, was fully aware of the sensitivity of his mission and took measures to ensure the safety of his ship – sentries were posted and steam was maintained in two rather than just one of the ship's boilers in case a quick getaway had to be made. Ammunition for some of the battleship's secondary armaments was kept ready and all visitors were carefully watched.

Below: The wreck of the USS Maine *after it was destroyed by an explosion in Havana harbor in February 1898.*

Shortly after Sigsbee retired to his cabin at 2130 hours on the evening of February 15, the *Maine* was rocked by a violent explosion – powerful enough to smash the ship's powerplant and break windows in Havana town. Other officers then reported a second explosion a few moments after the first. Sigsbee decided to flood the ship's magazines to prevent further explosions, but the crew told him that water was pouring into the ship and the magazines were already flooding. Fires were also raging in a mess hall amidship. When he heard that the forward magazine was threatened by fire, Sigsbee gave the order to abandon ship. At the roll call taken later, it was found that there were only 94 survivors, 55 of them injured.

Investigators initially believed that a magazine had exploded by accident, but senior US government officials were looking for an excuse to declare war, and wanted to use the incident as a pretext to do so. After hearing the reports of the divers who had investigated the wreck, the official inquiry decided that an underwater mine had been responsible for the catastrophe. The divers reported that hull plates had been blown inward, suggesting an external source of the explosion. These findings were confirmed in 1911 when the *Maine* was raised.

The sinking of the *Maine* galvanized public opinion against Spain in the United States, and the rallying call "Remember Maine – to hell with Spain" was heard on all sides. On April 29, 1898, the US Congress declared war. The Spanish-American war, that was to end in a US victory, had begun.

LUSITANIA, ATLANTIC
MAY 7, 1915

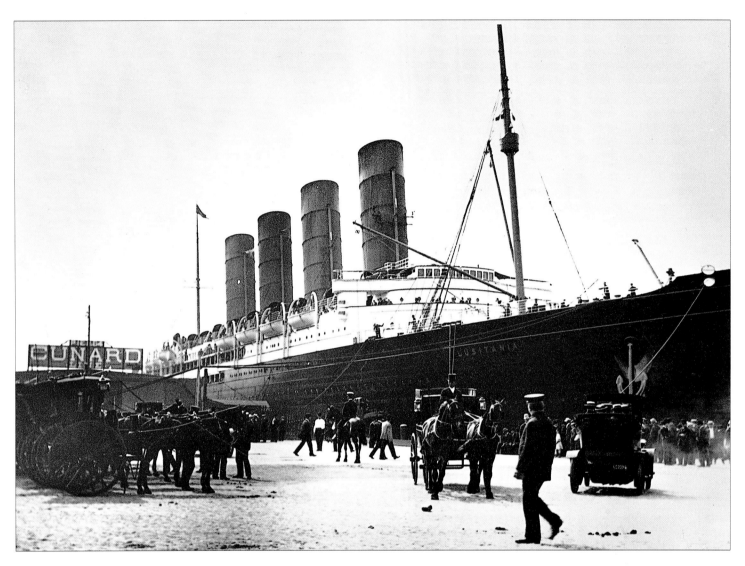

The sinking of the *Lusitania* in the second year of World War I was one of several incidents involving the loss of American lives that eventually led to the United States declaring war on Germany in 1917. The *Lusitania* was the first of the Cunard Line's great luxury liners and when it won its owners the Blue Riband for the fastest trans-atlantic crossing in 1909, the *Lusitania*'s future seemed secure. The crossing was completed at an average speed of just under 24 knots.

Although primarily a luxury passenger liner, the *Lusitania* had the potential to be much more. The ship had been designed in close cooperation with the British Admiralty. The Admiralty, suspecting that war with Germany was almost inevitable, demanded that Cunard build a fast ship laid out in such a way that it could be fitted with armaments. War was still some way off when, in May 1913, the *Lusitania* was given a secret refit – its port and starboard shelter decks were modified to take two four-gun batteries and room was made for two magazines to store the guns' ammunition. War was declared in August 1914 and by mid-September the *Lusitania* had been designated by the British Admiralty as an armed auxiliary cruiser.

The *Lusitania* continued to sail between Liverpool and New York as a passenger liner, despite Germany's declaration that the waters around Great Britain were a war zone and that any ship flying the British flag was likely to be sunk.

Above: The first of the Cunard Line's great luxury liners, the Lusitania *made its maiden voyage out of Liverpool, England, on September 7, 1907.*

Left: The first-class public rooms of the Lusitania – *such as the lounge shown here – were decorated in an opulent Edwardian style to encourage the passengers to think they were in the safety of a luxury hotel on dry land.*

The *Lusitania*'s final voyage began on May 1, 1915. The vessel was sailing from New York to Liverpool. On board were over 1150 passengers and 700 crew members, and 1400 tons of "general" cargo. Packed into the ship's holds, this included over 1200 cases of artillery shells and nearly 5000 boxes of cartridges.

Most of this cargo was positioned next to the bulkhead leading into the No. 1 boiler room, which had been converted into a magazine in 1913.

The ship's master, Captain William Turner, encountered no problems on the first part of the voyage back to Liverpool, and the ship made good time. However,

Left: The first-class dining room on the Lusitania.

Above: The Lusitania *went down less than 20 minutes after the first torpedo struck. Almost 1200 people perished.*

Far right: Half the Lusitania's *lifeboats could not be launched, and there was not enough room in the remaining boats for everybody on board.*

on May 6, the Admiralty in London began to send out warning messages regarding German submarine activity in the Irish Sea, which the *Lusitania* had to sail through to reach its home port.

Turner set in motion the established safety procedures – the liner's lifeboats were readied for evacuating passengers, extra lookouts were posted around the ship, portholes were covered up, and many watertight doors were closed.

On May 7, Captain Walter Schwieger of the U-boat U-20 spotted the *Lusitania* as it sailed off the Old Head of Kinsale. The liner was, unusually, sailing in a straight line rather than zigzagging. Shortly after 1400 hours the U-20 launched a single torpedo, which hit the *Lusitania* on its starboard side close to the bridge and near the bulkhead leading into the No.1 boiler room. Water flooded into the starboard coal bunkers and the ship took on a list. The *Lusitania* was then rocked by a second explosion caused by the detonation of its cargo of ammunition.

There was little panic among the passengers, although the ship was listing so badly that it was impossible to launch the boats on that side. When the passengers rushed to the other side, they found there were not enough lifeboats to accommodate them all. The *Lusitania* sank in less than 20 minutes from the first explosion, and many people went down with the ship or were lost in the sea. Over 700 passengers perished and only 289 of the crew survived the ordeal. Among the losses were 124 US citizens. The news of

Above: Two decades after the sinking, the wreck of the Lusitania *was found and photographed on the seabed by an American diver.*

the sinking of the *Lusitania* with the loss of civilian lives was blazed across newspapers around the world.

Both the US and British governments investigated the sinking of the liner. The US board of inquiry concluded that the loss was "an illegal act of the Imperial German government." However, the German authorities responded that the *Lusitania* had been warned of the dangers of sailing in Irish waters, that it was an auxiliary cruiser, and carrying war goods and, most remarkably, Canadian troops.

The British conceded that the liner had been converted to carry armaments, but said it was not doing so at the time of the sinking. Surviving passengers claimed to have seen no evidence that the ship was mounting guns or carrying Canadian troops. Later commentators speculated that the British government was actively seeking the destruction of the *Lusitania* as the loss of US lives would bring the United States closer to war with Germany. But no concrete evidence has ever been presented to support this theory.

ANCONA, ATLANTIC

NOVEMBER 8, 1915

Passenger liners sailing in time of war are at risk, particularly if they are owned by a line from one of the warring nations. The tragedy of the Italian-owned *Ancona*, which was sunk by a German submarine, was that Italy was not at war with Germany in November 1915.

The *Ancona*, owned by the Genoa-based Italia Società di Navigazione a Vapore, set sail on its last voyage from Naples on November 6 heading for New York. On the 8th the passenger ship was spotted by a submarine which, although actually German, was flying the Austrian flag. The submarine gave chase and slowly closed on the unsuspecting *Ancona*. The captain of the submarine could have used his deck gun to bring the ship to a halt, and allow the passengers and crew to escape before sinking the vessel. Instead, the submarine fired torpedoes at the defenceless liner.

The *Ancona* was hit at about 1300 hours. The damage was extensive and there was no hope of saving the vessel. The order was given to abandon the ship, which sank rapidly. Many made good their escape but 194 people died. The survivors were finally picked up by a French warship, the *Pluton*.

Eleven US nationals were among the dead and their government demanded an explanation from Austria. It then became clear that the submarine had in fact been a German boat, the U-38. This episode hardened US opinion against Germany and brought the United States closer to declaring war.

Above: The Italian passenger liner the Ancona, *which was torpedoed and sunk by a German U-boat in November 1915.*

MONT BLANC, HALIFAX

DECEMBER 7, 1917

By any standards, this incident ranks of one of the worst shipping disasters of the 20th century. Although it occurred during World War I, the destruction of the *Mont Blanc* – together with other ships and a sizeable part of the Canadian port of Halifax – owed nothing to enemy action.

The French cargo ship, the *Mont Blanc*, left New York early in December 1917 carrying a cargo consisting of TNT, benzene, picric acid, and gun cotton – an unstable and potentially lethal mix. The *Mont Blanc* sighted Halifax harbor at 0900 hours. on December 6.

Halifax is a natural deepwater harbor stretching for several miles. It is mostly more than one mile wide but narrows to just under half a mile at one point. As the *Mont Blanc* was being guided through the narrows by a pilot, crew members spotted a Belgian freighter, the *Imo*, sailing towards them. The *Imo* should have passed the *Mont Blanc* to starboard but signaled that it would pass to port. The *Mont Blanc*'s captain hauled his rudder over to avoid the other ship, but it was too late. The *Imo* crashed into the *Mont Blanc* close to the hold were the picric acid was stored.

The *Imo* was able to reverse away from the collision but was left unmaneuverable. Fire broke out on the *Mont Blanc*. Its crew abandoned the ship, and it began to drift toward Halifax. Some of the inhabitants of Halifax knew what cargo the *Mont Blanc* carried and how dangerous it was – and ran for their lives. A party from a British cruiser, the *High Flyer*, made an attempt to board the *Mont Blanc* and scuttle it. As they approached by ship's cutter, the *Mont Blanc* exploded.

The initial explosion was massive. Reports suggested that half of Halifax was flattened by it and the fire that followed. The impact of the explosive force was heightened by local geography. The land rose rapidly from the harbor, containing the force of the blast in a small area. Many were killed at the town's railroad station, which was wrecked. The homes of the dock workers around the harbor collapsed like a pack of cards, burying everyone inside.

The horror of the explosion was matched by the fire that followed. It spread rapidly across Halifax, engulfing two nearby areas, Dartmouth and Richmond. Another vessel, the *Pictou*, was moored in the harbor. It, too, carried ammunition. Remarkably, the *Pictou* survived the destruction of the *Mont Blanc* and thelikelihood of a second explosion from its cargo was averted when the freighter's sea-cocks were opened and the ship flooded.

Below: The Imo *aground in the landlocked harbor of Halifax after the explosion of the* Mont Blanc.

Right: The railroad station at Halifax was wrecked by the explosion.

The final list of casualties was enormous. Whole areas of housing were destroyed and by the end of the day there were an estimated 25,000 people left without homes in the depths of a Canadian winter. The number of dead was put at between 2000 and 3000, and some 8000 were treated for a variety of injuries. The center of Halifax was a shambles – most of its wooden buildings had been flattened or consumed by fire.

Right: Most of the timber-built houses of Halifax were destroyed by the blast from the explosion. Many of them collapsed, crushing those inside.

WILHELM GUSTLOFF, BALTIC SEA

JANUARY 30, 1945

The 25,484-ton passenger liner *Wilhelm Gustloff* was built by Blohm and Voss, Hamburg, and launched in 1938. The ship had been commissioned by the German Nazi Party's "Strength Through Joy" program, and it was named after a Swiss Nazi leader who had been assassinated in 1936. Intended to give German workers low-cost cruises, it was the first ship built especially for this program, and for this reason it had only one class of accommodation.

Before the *Wilhelm Gustloff* could start on its intended role as a vacation cruise ship, World War II broke out, and the ship was assigned to the German navy to serve as a troop ship and hospital ship in the Baltic Sea. At the beginning of 1945, the *Wilhelm Gustloff* was acting – along with several other ships – as a rescue ship in the massive evacuation of troops and refugees from the Baltic ports beseiged by the advancing Red Army.

Above: *The* Wilhelm Gustloff *was launched on May 5, 1938, in the presence of Adolf Hitler.*

Left: *Although built as a cruise ship, the* Wilhelm Gustloff *was never used in that role.*

At noon on January 30 the *Wilhelm Gustloff* sailed out of the port of Gdynia, Poland, crammed with about 6000 refugees and wounded servicemen. Just after 2100 hours the ship was struck by three torpedoes from a Soviet submarine, and sank almost immediately. Only about 500 people survived – the exact death toll is not known, but it must have been around 5500 making this the worst loss of life recorded in maritime history.

GRAND CAMP, TEXAS CITY

APRIL 16, 1947

A port can be a dangerous place. When ships carrying combustible or explosive cargoes are docked alongside each other, a single outbreak of fire can lead to a chain reaction. This was the case in the horrific disaster at Texas City in April 1947. When a fire broke out on the French freighter *Grand Camp* while it was in dock, it resulted in an explosion that wrecked numerous other ships, destroyed a chemical plant, and left an estimated 90 percent of Texas City, a key port on the Gulf of Mexico, in ruins. Some 800 fatalities were recorded by the Red Cross, but the final death toll was probably much higher. The area was declared a disaster zone, so great was the catastrophe.

Texas City was a major terminal for oil tankers, but the *Grand Camp* was carrying a potentially more lethal cargo – highly combustible ammonium nitrate, a white crystalline solid used in the manufacture of fertilizers and explosives.

Fire broke out on the *Grand Camp* in the early morning of April 16 and spread so quickly that the crew had no time to alert the harbor authorities. The fire took a firm hold on the vessel and ignited the ammonium nitrate in its hold. The chemical vaporized and produced an enormous explosion that obliterated the *Grand Camp*, flinging burning debris high into the air and across the harbor. The burning debris landed on the various buildings in the harbor and on many of

Below: Huge plumes of black, toxic smoke still linger over the port of Texas City the day after the Grand Camp with its cargo of ammonium nitrate exploded.

Right: Two women kneel to pray in the remains of the shattered Catholic church in Texas City. About 90 percent of the city was destroyed by the series of explosions set off by the Grand Camp.

Below: An emergency first aid station was set up to treat victims of the explosion.

the 50 or so oil tankers that were loading oil at the time. These tankers also began to burn out of control, spreading flames even farther afield. Thick plumes of acrid smoke soon blanketed the city in toxic fumes.

The fire continued to spread, quickly reaching a chemical plant. The city's overstretched fire department and rescue services were simply swamped by the magnitude of the disaster that confronted them. They tried hard to prevent the fires from spreading but with little success – the blaze continued out of control for several days. On the day after the initial explosion and fire, a second cargo vessel, the *High Flyer*, also blew up, adding to the carnage.

Much of Texas City was left in ruins. The initial blast flattened many of its wooden and brick buildings and the subsequent fires destroyed many more. It was even reported that a two-seater light aircraft flying over the harbor at the moment of detonation was a victim of the catastrophe. So powerful was the first explosion that there were reports of windows being smashed more than 10 miles (16km) from the point of detonation.

The devastation was horrific. A combination of explosive and combustible materials had torn the heart out of the city. It took many years – and millions of dollars – to restore the city to its position as one of the major ports on the Gulf of Mexico.

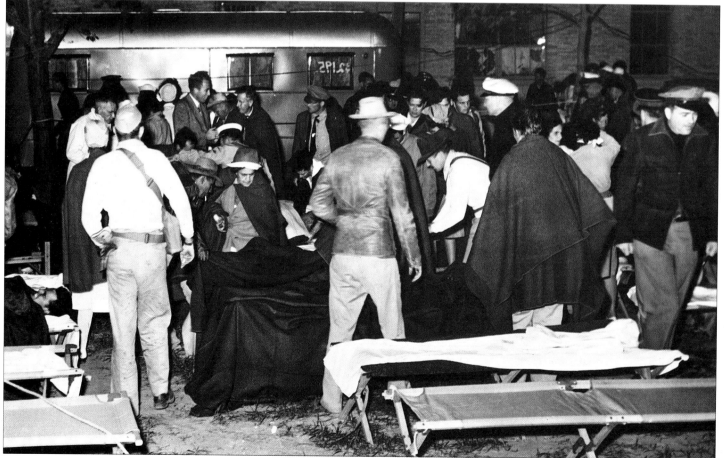

DARA, PERSIAN GULF

APRIL 8, 1961

Ships can be tempting targets for terrorists. When an explosion – followed by fire – sank the *Dara* in the Persian Gulf there was no thought initially that this was due to sabotage. But when divers went down to examine the wreck they found evidence of a bomb. The device had exploded in a passageway just above the *Dara*'s engine room, sending out a large fireball that engulfed parts of the ship.

The final voyage of the *Dara* began on March 23. The ship's master, Captain Elson, had 600 passengers on board. The outward leg to Basra went without a hitch and Elson then began the return trip, stopping at Korramshahr, Kuwait, and Bahrain before reaching Dubai on April 7. Elson took on more passengers and then decided to leave harbor early. The weather was worsening – there were gale-force winds and heavy hailstorms – and the vessel would be safer at sea. By the early morning of April 8 the weather had improved and the *Dara* turned back to Dubai.

At 0445 hours the *Dara* was rocked by an explosion, which stopped the engines and put the steering out of action. Frightened passengers and crew began to abandon ship – as the flames spread rapidly, many people threw themselves into the Gulf waters. A converted landing craft, the *Empire Guillemot*, saw the flames, sent out a distress signal (the *Dara*'s communication system had been put out of action), and rushed to the *Dara*'s aid.

Three British frigates also hastened to help the stricken ship, and managed to put out the flames.

Although more than 580 people were rescued, 241 others died in the disaster. An attempt was made to tow the *Dara* to port, but the ship sank on April 10.

Left: A survivor from the Dara *is put into an ambulance after being brought ashore from a rescue ship.*

Left: The British liner Dara, *owned by the British India Steam Navigation Company, was in the Persian Gulf when an explosion rocked the ship, putting it out of action.*

HUMAN ERROR

No one is infallible, but those who carry the responsibility of transporting passengers or dangerous cargoes by ship are expected to be so. Captains of vessels and their officers have a double responsibility – for the safety of the passengers and crew aboard, and for the safety of the cargo. All officers who put to sea are expected to be fully competent and experienced and to know every aspect of their job down to the smallest, often seemingly insignificant, detail. However, ships are not only complicated pieces of machinery. They are also small communities. And like communities on land, they are filled with human beings of differing abilities and weaknesses.

Sailors do make mistakes. It might be due to laziness, a momentary lapse of concentration, neglect, or downright disobedience to an order or safety procedure. In some cases mistakes are genuinely made and those involved often show sincere regret and grief at the tragedy their actions have caused. In one of the cases described here, a captain committed suicide after he allowed his ship to run aground.

Others have had to be brought to justice by boards of inquiry. Painstaking investigation of the causes of a disaster, scientific analysis, and a dogged determination to get at the truth rarely allow the guilty to escape justice. However, it is not just captains and their crews who may be culpable. Shipping lines and their top executives have had to answer charges relating to their conduct and business activities. Perhaps the biggest bone of contention at the present time is the use of flags of convenience from countries where the strict safety requirements of other countries are less rigorously enforced.

Right: Following the Exxon Valdez *disaster, in which over 11 million gallons (50 million litres) of crude oil were spilled in Prince William Sound, Alaska, a massive clean-up and rescue operation was mounted to try to save wildlife in the area. But help came too late for these sea otters covered in oil.*

HMS VICTORIA, MEDITERRANEAN

JUNE 22, 1893

The loss of HMS *Victoria* in the eastern Mediterranean in 1893 remains the worst peacetime disaster that the British Royal Navy has ever suffered. The 10,740-ton *Victoria* was launched in 1887 and was something of an experimental ship. At the time of the sinking the warship was armed with two guns each weighing 111 tons. These were so heavy that their barrels tended to droop down under their own weight and it was believed unwise to fire them with their full charges of powder.

The loss of the *Victoria* was in large part due to the misjudgment of one man, Vice-Admiral Sir George Tyron. Tyron, who was commander-in-chief of the Royal Navy's Mediterranean Fleet at the time of the sinking, was an experienced officer. He had commanded the navy's first ironclad warship, the *Warrior*, and was considered a naval warfare expert.

The *Victoria* was Tyron's flagship on the day of its sinking. Tyron had split the fleet in two and was carrying out maneuvers. The *Victoria* and the other vessel involved in the incident, HMS *Camperdown*, were each leading their respective halves of the fleet. Tyron ordered the two lines of ships to turn towards each other. The captains of both leading vessels complied with his order, yet it was plain to many watching that the two ships were far too close to each other for them to complete the change in direction without colliding.

The two ship did collide and the *Victoria* sank with the loss of 359 men, including Tyron himself. Fortunately the other vessels of the fleet were on hand to rescue the 284 survivors.

Below: HMS Victoria, *the flagship of the British Mediterranean Fleet, sinking after colliding with the* Camperdown *while carrying out maneuvers off Tripoli.*

GENERAL SLOCUM, NEW YORK

JUNE 15, 1904

Every shipwreck involving the loss of life is a tragedy, but the destruction of the sidewheel ferry *General Slocum* and the huge loss of life that accompanied it had a profound impact on the American people. The disaster seemed the more terrible because the ferry was packed with New Yorkers heading away from the heat of the city to enjoy a summer picnic. A large party of school children from St Mark's School, along with their teachers and parents, were among the passengers.

The *General Slocum* was a large vessel and it was packed to capacity when it sailed out from New York. It was under charter and its destination was Throg's Neck, a popular spot to pass away a pleasant summer's day. As the ferry, commanded by Captain van Schaick, made its way down the East River; those on board were totally unaware that disaster was about to strike. Most of the passengers watched the New York skyline pass, enjoying the cool breeze generated by the ship's progress down the river.

Eyewitness reports differ as to the source of the fire that engulfed the ship. Everybody seemed to agree that it started below deck. Some witnesses stated that the fire began in the ship's galley, the source being a stove; others reported that it started in a paint store. Whatever the truth of the matter, the fire spread rapidly throughout the wooden ship.

Within minutes the ship was in difficulties, but the crew members detailed to fight the fire stuck to their impossible task for nearly one hour. There was no saving the vessel, however, and those caught on board faced a terrible dilemma. They could stay with the *General Slocum* and hope the flames could be brought under control, or they could take their chance in the waters of the East River. Some jumped for their lives, but many of these drowned. Most stayed with the ship and perished in the flames.

The vessel – what was left of it after it the superstructure had been burnt to the waterline – eventually sank. The final tally of dead was 1021 passengers and crew – but the true figure may have been higher than this as no one really knew how many people were actually on board.

A disaster of such magnitude was, of course, investigated by the authorities. Captain van Schaick had survived the inferno and played a key role in the investigations. When the board of inquiry delivered its verdict, he was singled out as being at least partially responsible for the catastrophe. He was subsequently

tried and convicted on a charge of manslaughter, and received a jail term. So great was the grief of ordinary New Yorkers that the city erected a plaque to commemorate the sinking of the *General Slocum*.

Above: Horrified passengers jump from the burning General Slocum.

67

PRINZESSIN VICTORIA LUISE, CARIBBEAN

DECEMBER 16, 1906

The **Prinzessin Victoria Luise** was built for the Hamburg American Line and was originally fitted out to cater for up to 200 wealthy passengers who were willing to pay well for cruising the Mediterranean in considerable luxury. However, the **Prinzessin Victoria Luise** was pressed into service on the Hamburg–New York run when the vessel's owners needed extra ships to cater for the boom in transatlantic travel.

The *Prinzessin Victoria Luise* had made only six round trip crossings of the Atlantic before disaster struck. On December 12, 1906, the vessel reverted to carrying wealthy passengers on cruises, sailing out of New York bound for Jamaica. The outward journey passed without incident and the ship then headed for home. The captain, H. Brunswig, was sailing without a pilot, and he himself plotted the course along the Jamaican coast that the vessel was to follow during the night of December 16.

On that night the *Prinzessin Victoria Luise* ran aground on rocks close to the lighthouse near Port Royal. The passengers panicked, as they fully expected the ship to go down immediately. They were reassured by crew members and transferred to shore without mishap. The *Prinzessin Victoria Luise* was, however, stuck fast. When a storm blew up on the afternoon of the next day, the ship began to break up. The captain, knowing that he should have had a pilot on board rather than sail the waters alone, retired to his cabin, locked the doors, and blew out his brains. He was the only casualty of the disaster.

Above: The luxury liner Prinzessin Victoria Luise *stranded near Plumb Point lighthouse, Kingston, Jamaica. The ship ran aground on December 16, 1906, and after a storm it broke up.*

DAKOTA, PACIFIC
MARCH 7, 1907

The *Dakota* was the pride of the US Great Northern Steam Ship Company. At over 20,700 gross tons, the *Dakota* was 630 feet (191m) long, and had accommodation for 2700 passengers. The ship was the biggest US-constructed passenger vessel when it was commissioned in 1905, a record that was to stand until the late 1920s. However, the *Dakota*'s career was destined to be brief.

The *Dakota*, along with the *Minnesota*, was the brainchild of the owner of the Great North Railroad, James Hill. He saw a gap in the market on the United States–Far East run. Both the *Dakota* and its sister ship the *Minnesota* were built to transport the passengers and freight being carried on his railroad to and from the Far East. As a concession to the tastes of his Oriental passengers, Hill ordered an opium den to be built on both ships.

The *Dakota*'s life came to an end on March 7, 1907. The ship had sailed from the Pacific Northwest and was heading for Japan. It never completed the journey. Some 40 miles (64km) out from Yokohama, the main port of Tokyo Bay and the first Japanese port opened to Westerners in the 19th century, the *Dakota* struck a submerged reef. The ship was stuck fast and the passengers and crew were able to abandon it without mishap. A storm on March 23 put paid to all hopes of saving the ship, however. It broke up during the pounding and was sold for scrap.

The captain, whether out of guilt or shock, gave up his life at sea, and took a job for the remainder of his life as a guard in a San Francisco shipyard.

Right: One of the last photographs taken of the Dakota *as it sinks 40 miles (64km) off Yokohama.*

MORRO CASTLE, ATLANTIC

SEPTEMBER 8, 1934

The fate of the *Morro Castle* was a classic example of how incompetence and negligence can result in unnecessary loss of life. When the *Morro Castle* caught fire it was only six miles off the coast of New Jersey. Yet the confusion that reigned on board led to the loss of 137 lives – and a series of expensive law suits for payment of damages. Another result was that new regulations governing safety at sea were brought in for US ships.

The *Morro Castle* was built to transport passengers between New York and Havana and undertook its maiden voyage out of New York on August 23, 1930.

Some four years later, in September 1934, the *Morro Castle* was nearing the end of the homeward voyage with 316 passengers and 231 crew members on board.

The captain, Captain Robert Wilmott, appears to have been a rather paranoid character. He was reportedly convinced that someone was out to do him harm and so isolated himself, staying either on the bridge or in his cabin.

Wilmott never made it back to New York alive – he died from a suspected heart attack during the night of September 7 and was replaced by Chief Officer William Warms. When Warms took over command of the liner, it was negotiating heavy seas and strong winds. At

Left: When the acting captain gave the order to abandon ship, many of the first people into the lifeboats were members of the crew.

Above: The still-smoldering Morro Castle *lies beached in front of Convention Hall, Asbury Park, New Jersey.*

Right: A coast-guard returns from the charred remains of the beached Morro Castle *carrying the body of a child found dead on the wreck.*

about 0200 hours on the morning of September 8 a passenger found a fire in a writing room. He called a steward, who attempted to put out the fire. Unfortunately the steward failed to notify the bridge about the problem. About 60 minutes passed before Warms heard of the fire, by which time it had spread alarmingly due to the ship's wooden panelling and the strong winds that were blowing. To make matters worse, the ship was short of the correct number of firehoses, and those that were available had to be dragged some distance to fight the fires. Many of the water points had been capped, making them unusable.

There had been no fire or boat drill during the voyage, so neither the passengers nor the crew members knew what to do in the emergency and confusion reigned. Warms was too inexperienced to follow correct procedures. He did not send out a distress call for some time, even though the fire was clearly getting out of hand. Distress signals were sent out eventually but these ceased when an explosion destroyed the generator.

The crew behaved badly once the evacuation got underway. Passengers and crew gathered at either the bow or stern as the central section of the ship was ablaze. The first lifeboat to get way held 92 crew members and only six passengers. Several vessels picked up the *Morro Castle*'s distress call and raced to the scene. These ships rescued many of the passengers, but 137 people died. The abandoned liner eventually drifted ashore at Asbury Park, New Jersey.

The subsequent board of investigation placed the blame for the catastrophe on the shoulders of the ship's owners and crew. Warms was found guilty of negligence and given two years in prison, the vessel's chief engineer, one of the first into a lifeboat, was jailed for five years, and the vice-president of the line was fined. Passengers received compensation.

HERAKLION, AEGEAN SEA

DECEMBER 8, 1966

Above: The Greek car ferry Heraklion *which sank midway between Crete and Piraeus with the loss of over 200 lives.*

Lax discipline and flouting of safety regulations on passenger ferry services generally only come to light after a tragedy has occurred. Such was the case with the Greek ferry *Heraklion*, which foundered in rough seas on its regular trip from Crete to Piraeus. A rescue vessel reached the site within 30 minutes but no trace of the ship was found. There was some debris and huge quantities of fruit floating on the rough seas, but no sign of the *Heraklion*. Later, 47 passengers and crew were found on the island of Falconcra but the remaining 231 were presumed lost. What had happened?

The 8,922-gross ton *Heraklion* had begun life as the *Leicestershire*, which sailed the British–Burma route, but was sold to Greece's Typaldos Lines in 1964 to sail between Piraeus and Crete. On December 7, 1966, the weather on the Aegean Sea was treacherous and

stormy. Nevertheless the *Heraklion* sailed out on the normal ferry service from Crete. The buffeting the ship took caused considerable problems on the cargo deck, loosening the ties that held cars and lorries. One 16-ton trailer broke loose and smashed into the cargo door, which opened the vessel to the raging waters outside. The *Heraklion* flooded rapidly. The vessel sent a distress signal at 0200 hours on December 8, and the Greek air force and navy, as well as two British warships, responded quickly. But their arrival was too late for most on board the *Heraklion*.

The loss of the ferry was investigated and the Typaldos Lines was severely criticized. The board reported that the ship did not have an established emergency drill, the SOS was sent out too late, and the ship's officers had failed in their duty. Charges of manslaughter and forgery were brought. Two of the company's senior officials were given jail sentences.

TORREY CANYON, ENGLISH CHANNEL

MARCH 18, 1967

Right: The super-tanker Torrey Canyon *breaking up after it ran aground on Seven Stones Rocks.*

The grounding of the *Torrey Canyon* super-tanker on Pollard Rock, the most western of the Seven Stones Rocks off England's Land's End, heralded a radical rethink on the dangers and methods of coping with oil spills at sea. When the calculations were made, it was estimated that around 100,000 tons of crude oil had leaked into the waters off England and France. This oil spill was 10 times greater than any previous spillage. Governments and anti-pollution agencies did not have any experience of dealing with an environmental catastrophe of this magnitude.

The 118,285-ton *Torrey Canyon* was sailing from the Persian Gulf for the Milford Haven oil terminal in south Wales. The tanker, captained by the experienced Pastrengo Rugiati, was sailing under a Liberian flag.

Although owned by the Barracuda Tanker Company of Bermuda, on its fateful voyage the *Torrey Canyon* was chartered for British Petroleum. Captain Rugiati was under a little pressure from the Milford Haven authorities. If he did not make the evening tide on March 18, it was unlikely that he and his valuable cargo would be able to dock until the 24th.

The incident began at 0630 hours, when one of the vessel's officers picked up a radar reflection off to starboard. He was expecting an echo off the Scilly Isles, but from port. He ordered a change in direction to take the vessel to the west of the radar echo, but Rugiati intervened, taking the *Torrey Canyon* back on to its original heading and – unusually – putting the ship on autopilot. A nearby lightship saw the danger and fired warning rockets but to no avail. The tanker hit Pollard Rock at 0915 hours. Rugiati ordered "full astern" but the ship was stuck fast. The sound of metal grinding on rock also suggested that its bottom was being torn out.

Over the following days efforts were made to pull the *Torrey Canyon* off Pollard Rock. None was successful, and after an explosion in the engine room left one crewman dead, the vessel was abandoned. As the weather worsened oil, which had only been seeping out of the damaged hull, began to pour out after the vessel broke its back on March 27. Aerial photographs revealed an oil slick some 35 miles (56km) long and up to 15 miles (24km) wide. Beaches in southwest England, Brittany, and the Channel Islands were coated in oil. Tourism was badly damaged and thousands of seabirds died. The fishing industry was also severely disrupted.

The authorities tried several methods to minimize the damage. Detergent was sprayed to break up the slick and booms were deployed to contain it. Finally, the Royal Air Force bombed the *Torrey Canyon* hoping to set fire to the oil remaining on board. None of these measures was wholly successful, although the first bombing mission did ignite some oil, which burned for two hours. The subsequent Liberian board of inquiry concluded that "the master [Rugiati] alone is responsible for this casualty." It recommended that Rugiati's captain's license be revoked because of his negligence and the severity of the incident.

Left: A helicopter lowers a large compressor on to the deck of the Torrey Canyon *as salvage crew work desperately in an attempt to refloat the tanker on the next high tide.*

Below: After the crew of the Torrey Canyon *had been evacuated, the RAF set fire to the oil on board, which burned for two hours sending out clouds of dense black smoke.*

EXXON VALDEZ, PRINCE WILLIAM SOUND

MARCH 24, 1989

Below: A tug pulls the damaged Exxon Valdez across Prince William Sound past floating ice.

Alaska is one of the Earth's last great wildernesses – it is also rich in oil deposits. The environmental cost of any oil spillage was brought home when the *Exxon Valdez*, a 211,469-ton VLCC (Very Large Crude Carrier) ran aground on Bligh Reef as it was making its way from the terminal at Valdez down Prince William Sound to the open waters of the Gulf of Alaska.

The *Exxon Valdez* was commanded by Captain Joseph Hazelwood and had a crew of 20. Hazelwood, although young, had 10 years of seafaring experience and had made the journey from Valdez on several occasions. As was usual, he took on board a pilot, Ed Murphy, shortly before leaving Valdez at 2100 hours on March 24. Murphy was present to guide the tanker down the Valdez Narrows and past the Valdez Arm, a distance of

some 20 miles (32km). This was accomplished shortly before 2330 hours and Murphy was dropped off at Rocky Point.

After disembarking Murphy, the captain spotted a number of small icebergs (growlers) in his path and gained permission from the Vessel Traffic Control Center to alter course slightly. He then handed over control of the *Exxon Valdez* to his third mate, Greg Cousins. Cousins was asked to take the ship through a narrow seaway between Busby Island and Bligh Reef. At midnight, the ship's helmsman changed watch and

Cousins agreed to be relieved some time later. A change of course was requested at the same time but investigators later discovered that this order was not implemented for a minute.

Two minutes after midnight Cousins, checking his radar, saw that the request to change course had not been carried out and ordered a change in the angle of the ship's rudder. The helmsman had been led to believe that the new heading would be between 235 and 245 degrees, not the 247 degrees ordered by Cousins, so stopped the rudder change early. Cousins

Right: Oil from the Exxon Valdez *is pumped into another tanker in an attempt to reduce the oil spill.*

Right: Cleaning up operations included the use of perforated hoses that sprayed sea water over the contaminated shorelines to wash the oil back into the sea. There it could be skimmed off with skimmers.

Below: In the port of Valdez, Alaska, workers begin the process of skimming the oil from the surface of the sea.

spotted that the tanker was dangerously close to Bligh Reef and contacted the captain. As he did so, the *Exxon Valdez* struck its rocks.

The vessel was holed and its cargo of oil began to spill into the channel. No one could guess the extent of the pollution that was to follow. Estimates indicate that over 11 million gallons (50 million liters) of oil escaped, polluting an area of 500 square miles (1300 sq km). Thick crude oil was washed ashore along over 800 miles (1300km) of Alaskan coastline.

The site of the spillage was remote and the wintry weather further complicated matters. To make things worse, one of the key anti-pollution vessels was out of action for two vital days and the air terminal building at Valdez was damaged by a storm two days after the grounding. The delays in getting the cleaning-up operation started were costly. Two weeks after the incident only around 20 percent of the spilled oil had been recovered or contained with booms and the vast oil slick was stretching up to 70 miles (115km) from the tanker. More than 30,000 seabirds as well as many mammals are thought to have died from the pollution.

Hazelwood was acquitted on charges of criminal negligence in the US but the court stated that the accident would probably not have happened if he had stayed on the *Exxon Valdez* bridge. Exxon itself was held responsible and ordered to foot the bill for the clean-up operation.

HERALD OF FREE ENTERPRISE, ZEEBRUGGE

MARCH 6, 1987

The cross-Channel ferry service was, even before the opening of the Channel Tunnel rail link, a highly competitive business. Townsend Thoresen, one of the big operators, took over the P&O Group in April 1987 and as part of the deal gained a number of RO-RO (roll-on, roll-off) ferries, including the 7591-ton *Herald of Free Enterprise*.

Roll-on, roll-off ferries carry coaches, lorries, and cars across the English Channel, and are fitted with massive doors at both bow and stern to speed up the loading and unloading processes. A quick turn-around is vital to profitability. The *Herald of Free Enterprise* usually worked between Dover and Calais but was transferred

to the Zeebrugge run early in March to take the place of another ferry that was undergoing maintenance. On March 6, the *Herald* left Dover at 1130 hours. The crossing, which went without a hitch, was completed by late afternoon. There was meant to be a two-hour stay at Zeebrugge, loading passengers and vehicles. The *Herald* was due to depart on its return leg at about 1730 hours, but was delayed because of time it took to process a large, unseasonable number of passengers taking advantage of a cheap-crossing promotion.

Zeebrugge harbor is somewhat confined and ferries have to maneuver carefully to reach open water. The *Herald* had to reverse stern first into a side-dock and then, bow-first, head out into the Channel. The *Herald*

Left: *When the car ferry* Herald of Free Enterprise *rolled over just outside Zeebrugge harbor, many passengers were trapped inside and drowned.*

Left: Giant barge cranes pull the Herald of Free Enterprise *upright before the ferry is towed away.*

accomplished the first stage of the maneuver but disaster struck as it moved forward. The main bow door, giving entrance to the car deck had been left open. As the ship moved forward at around 18 knots, tons of water were scooped up and entered the deck. As the ship rolled, the water also rolled from side to side, setting up a lateral motion that sent the vessel over on to its port side in less than a minute. It came to rest on a sandbank just outside the port's outer breakwater.

Chaos reigned inside the stricken vessel. Passengers below deck panicked as they fought to get out before being drowned. The lights went out and water continued to flood into the vessel. Belgian rescue services were quickly on the scene of the disaster and began to rescue the crew and passengers. Some 408 were brought out alive almost immediately, along with 50 bodies. The final death toll reached nearly 200. The *Herald* was eventually righted by a Dutch salvage company, Smit International, and then sailed to the Far East, where it was scrapped.

The board of inquiry found Townsend Thoresen wholly responsible for the disaster. In particular, it noted that several of the company's captains had already expressed their disquiet over the regulations for closing doors, and that there was no means for a captain to check for himself that the doors were shut. The inquiry stated that the company's management was "infected with the disease of sloppiness from top to bottom". Ferries were henceforth to be fitted with an indicator light to show whether doors were open or closed.

Left: A frogman in a dinghy inspects the open bow doors of the capsized ferry. Netting was hung over the opening to prevent cargo escaping.

SEA EMPRESS, OFF WELSH COAST

FEBRUARY 15, 1996

The Pembrokeshire coastline of South Wales is one of the most scenically outstanding in the British Isles. It is also home to a large population of grey seals and thousands of seabirds, including widgeon, shelduck, curlew, teal, and redshank. All this was to be severely threatened on the evening of February 15, 1996.

On that Thursday evening, at about 2000 hours, a 147,000-ton oil tanker called the *Sea Empress* was approaching Milford Haven estuary on the South Wales coast, carrying 128,000 tons of crude North Sea oil. The Liberian-registered tanker, with its 28-man Russian crew, was headed for the Texaco oil refinery further along the estuary. With a pilot on board, the giant 1300-feet (400-m) long tanker was negotiating the entrance to the estuary when it hit submerged rocks and ran aground. The hull was holed, and crude oil began leaking out into the sea.

Rescue tugs and anti-pollution craft raced to the scene, and within two hours the tanker was refloated. However, a gale was blowing up, and crude oil was

Above: A bird specialist holds a rescued red throated diver covered with oil from the Sea Empress.

Above: *The super-tanker* Sea Empress *ran aground on submerged rocks off Cape Ann's Head on February 15. Despite repeated attempts to refloat the vessel, the tanker was not finally towed into Milford Haven until six days later. Meanwhile 70,000 tons of crude oil leaked from the ship.*

continuing to leak from the vessel. The crew – none of whom had been injured – remained on board the stricken tanker and attempted to pump oil out of the damaged tanks into undamaged ones.

Over the weekend the weather worsened, and during high winds on the Saturday night the towlines snapped and the *Sea Empress* ran aground for the second time. There were fears that the petroleum vapors might ignite, and the crew were taken off by RAF rescue helicopters. For the next few days salvage operations were hampered by gale-force winds, and meanwhile oil continued to leak from the tanker, spreading along the Pembrokeshire coastline covering beaches and rocks with black slime and endangering the wildlife. Oil slicks were also moving towards the bird sanctuaries of the Skomer and Skokholm islands to the west.

A massive cleaning up operation was mounted, with pollution experts spraying dispersant chemicals from the air over a 12-mile (19-km) oil slick. In all, about 70,000 tons of crude oil were released.

After further abortive attempts to recover the tanker, the *Sea Empress* was finally towed into Milford Haven on Wednesday, February 21, six days after it first ran aground. The vessel was still leaking oil. Six weeks later the tanker was taken to a Belfast shipyard for repairs.

Above: Tugs battle with gale force winds in an effort to free the grounded tanker from the rocks.

Left: A Dakota plane sprays detergent over the sea to break up the oil while a helicopter hovers over the tanker prior to dropping pumps to help transfer the oil to undamaged tanks.

WEATHER AND MECHANICAL FAILURE

Ships at sea often have to cope with the immense stresses created by giant waves, hurricane force winds, and tropical storms. Even the largest and most strongly built vessels can be buffeted to destruction by the uncontrolled forces of nature. The rolling motions encountered on the high seas can also have a devastating impact on a ship by endangering the security of its cargo. Once cargoes have broken free they can be swept from side to side within a ship's hold and eventually flip the ship over on to its side.

Disasters in bad weather also make the evacuation of a vessel and the rescue of survivors by other ships extremely difficult. Passengers are more likely to panic in poor weather conditions and the difficulties of launching lifeboats are much greater in heavy seas. Many passengers and lifeboats have simply disappeared because they were swamped by monumental waves or blanketed by thick fog.

Mechanical failure is not uncommon in ships and on occasion can be so cataclysmic that it can send a vessel to the bottom. Even regular maintenance and a continuous watch over machinery cannot guarantee that mechanical failures will not occur.

Right: The German liner Hanseatic *setting sail from Southampton. This great liner was to be destroyed while in dock in New York harbor by the failure of a small component that led to a catastrophic fire.*

PRINCIPESSA MAFALDA, ATLANTIC

OCTOBER 25, 1927

Right: As the holed Principessa Mafalda *settles in the water, the lifeboats are launched and the ship's passengers and crew try to escape. Even so, over 300 people perished when the ship went down.*

The luxury liner *Principessa Mafalda* was built in 1909 and could carry up to 1700 passengers (in two classes) and around 300 crew at a top speed of 16 knots. The ship plied the lucrative route to South America, chiefly Buenos Aires, from both Naples and Genoa for the Lloyd Italiano line until the company was bought by the Italian Navigazione Generale Italiana in June 1918.

The *Principessa Mafalda*'s last voyage was supposed to take it to Rio de Janeiro but the vessel never reached its intended destination. Leaving the Cape Verde Islands on October 8 for the final leg of its journey, the *Principessa Mafalda* had 288 crew and 971 passengers on board. Disaster struck as the vessel was near to Abrolhos Island off the coast of Brazil on the morning of October 25. The shaft of the ship's port propeller broke off with considerable force. The damage caused to the immediate area was considerable, including a sizeable hole torn out of the hull. Water flooded into the engine room and quickly filled the boilers. The build-up of steam caused an explosion that blew the boilers to pieces.

The captain immediately signaled for help, but the *Principessa Mafalda* was already settling in the water and listing heavily to port. Seven vessels heeded the distress call and made all speed for the stricken liner. The *Principessa* survived for just under four hours after the explosion before capsizing, taking over 300 passengers and crew to the bottom.

VESTRIS, ATLANTIC

NOVEMBER 12, 1928

The ill-starred *Vestris* was commissioned by Lamport and Holt of Liverpool, England, and first put into service in 1912. At the time of its launch its owners had no idea that the vessel's loss 16 years later would be partly responsible for the company withdrawing from the lucrative service to New York. The 10,494-gross ton *Vestris* was built to carry up to 610 passengers, including 280 in first class, and had a top speed of 15 knots.

When it was first put into service the *Vestris* worked the route between New York and La Plata in South America, but it was then chartered by the Cunard Line and later Royal Mail Lines before being returned to Lamport and Holt in 1922. The fateful journey began on November 10, 1928. Captain W. Carey took his ship out of New York harbor and headed for Buenos Aires. On board were 197 crew and 129 passengers.

The *Vestris* soon encountered heavy seas due to the worsening weather, and the vessel developed a list. This would not have been too dangerous except that some of the ship's cargo and bunker coal began to shift because of the list. As the list increased, some 300 miles (480km) out from Hampton Roads, Carey ordered the sending of an SOS signal and placed the passengers and most of the crew in lifeboats.

Before all of them could be evacuated the *Vestris* went over, going to the bottom with 68 passengers and more than 40 of its crew. The prompt arrival of rescue ships, including the battleship USS *Wyoming* and the North German Lloyd Line liner *Berlin*, undoubtedly prevented the loss of life from being even greater.

Right: A picture taken aboard the Vestris *a few minutes before the liner sank, with the loss of over 100 lives.*

PAMIR, ATLANTIC
SEPTEMBER 21, 1957

The loss of the *Pamir* led to an outpouring of grief among the public of West Germany when news of its sinking was reported by the media. The 3103-ton *Pamir* was being used as a training vessel and was in the Atlantic, bound for Hamburg from Buenos Aires. On board were 86 crew members, 53 of them young naval cadets learning how to sail this famous four-masted windjammer.

The *Pamir* was built by Blohm and Voss in 1905 and was originally powered by sails from its four masts. As a sailing ship it became famous in the early years of the 20th century in the "grain races" from Australia.

In the early 1930s the *Pamir* was bought by a Finn, Captain Gustav Erikson, and in 1951 changed owners again. In 1954 the ship was taken over by the Pamir-Passat Foundation. Although the *Pamir* kept its sails it also now had auxiliary oil engines.

At the time of its loss the *Pamir* was acting as a training ship for German naval cadets. It was 600 miles southwest of the Azores when it ran into a hurricane. The final message received from the ship said that the sails were ripped to shreds, the foremast had snapped off, and the ship was listing 45 degrees. That was the last that was ever heard of the *Pamir*. Of the 86 crew members on board, only six survived the ordeal.

Above: *Karl Otto Dummer, one of six survivors from the* Pamir, *greets his family on his safe arrival at Frankfurt.*

Left: *The four-masted German windjammer, the* Pamir.

HANSEATIC, NEW YORK

SEPTEMBER 7, 1966

As the loss of the *Hanseatic* proves, a ship does not have to be on the high seas to suffer a major catastrophe. The *Hanseatic* was lying peacefully at anchor in New York harbor when the failure of a small component in the engine room led to a fire that swiftly engulfed the ship. It was the end of a 30,000-ton vessel that had, as a troopship, survived the horrors of World War II.

The *Hanseatic* began life as the *Empress of Japan*, plying between Vancouver and Yokohama in Japan. War brought an understandable change of name to the *Empress of Scotland* in 1942. Released back to civilian use in 1948, the ship was eventually bought by the Hamburg-Atlantic Line early in 1958 and renamed the *Hanseatic*. The *Hanseatic*'s main route was between Germany and New York but it was also employed as a

winter cruise ship. The vessel was destroyed shortly before it was due to set out on one of these cruises on that fateful September 7. Only three of the scheduled 425 passengers were on board the *Hanseatic* when fire broke out at about 0730 hours. If the fire had started later, nearer the 1130 hours sailing time, more passengers would have been on board and the loss of life might have been considerable.

The fire started in the engine room and was caused by either a broken gasket or a faulty fuel line. Whatever the cause, the flames took hold rapidly, spreading into two more engine rooms and making their way undetected via vents to the passenger decks. The fire was eventually brought under control, but the damage was too extensive to make repair an economically viable option. The *Hanseatic* was finally towed to Hamburg and sold for scrap in December 1966.

Above: The Hanseatic on fire in New York harbor. The 500 crew members and the three passengers aboard were all evacuated safely.

WAHINE, NEW ZEALAND

APRIL 11, 1968

A shipwreck can have profound repercussions for its passengers, crew, the vessel itself, and its owners. The loss of the 8948-gross ton *Wahine* in April 1968 left more than 50 people dead or missing. The ship was fit for nothing but scrap, and the disaster sparked a chain of events that led to the closure of the ship's parent company, the Union Steamship Company of New Zealand. This venerable company, which had been founded in 1875, had its reputation ruined by the incident.

The *Wahine*, with room for more than 900 passengers, was a hard-working vessel. Built in Glasgow in 1966 by Fairfield Limited, it was earmarked to carry passengers and cars between Wellington on New Zealand's North Island and Lyttelton on the South Island. It was expected to make six overnight crossings between the two ports each week. The seas around New Zealand were well known for ferocious storms.

On April 11 the *Wahine* was making its way to Wellington in the teeth of a ferocious gale with winds gusting at over 120mph (192km/h). There was zero visibility. The ship struggled to maintain its course, but its captain and helmsman found it increasingly difficult to keep control of the *Wahine*. Shortly after 0630 hours the vessel was thrown on to the sharp rocks of Barretts Reef close to the entrance to Wellington harbor. Somehow the *Wahine* broke free of the reef but the damage had been done – the hull was holed and the starboard propeller had been severed.

Reports from the engine room indicated that water was flooding in. If the vessel could not reach a safe

Below: The Wahine *at midday on April 11. The ship has been damaged and is listing to starboard, and the first lifeboats are being launched.*

anchorage, it would undoubtedly founder. During the attempt to find safer waters, the *Wahine* was again thrown on to rocks at the entrance to a channel known as Chaffers Passage. There was no saving the vessel. Water poured through the twisted and torn hull plates causing the *Wahine* to heel over to starboard.

At 1330 hours the order to abandon ship was given. As the *Wahine*'s port-side lifeboats were unusable because of the list, those on board – more than 700 passengers and crew – had to take to the lifeboats on the starboard side. Reports indicate that there was some panic but matters eased when the violent winds subsided. Although the seas were still rough, the evacuation was carried out with a degree of control for the most part. Nevertheless, 50 lives were lost.

What of the vessel itself? The *Wahine* eventually rolled over completely on to its starboard side and was declared a total wreck. Repair costs were far too high to make restoring the ship worthwhile. The *Wahine* was righted and refloated, but then sold for scrap.

The Union Steamship Company finally got around to replacing the *Wahine* in 1972, but failed to recognize the change in public opinion that followed the disaster. New Zealanders turned to other forms of transport to commute between Lyttelton and Wellington. In 1974 the Union Steamship Company folded.

Left: The day after the disaster the capsized Wahine *lies on its side in Wellington harbor.*

Right: Survivors from the Wahine *are brought ashore in a lifeboat. Over 50 people were lost in the disaster.*

PATRA, RED SEA

DECEMBER 25, 1976

The 3920-ton *Patra* began life as *Kronprins Frederik* in 1941, but because of World War II the ship did not make its first commercial voyage until 1946. The *Kronprins Frederik* was a fine, speedy vessel that worked routes between England and Denmark until it was sold to Arab Navigators in 1976 and renamed the *Patra*.

The new owners quickly put the *Patra* into service as a roll-on, roll-off ferry operating between Jedda in Saudi Arabia and Suez in Egypt. It could carry more than 350 passengers. The vessel's final voyage began at Jedda on December 25, 1976. On board were crowds of Muslim pilgrims returning to Egypt after having made the pilgrimage to the holy city of Mecca. Some 50 miles (80km) and five hours out from Jedda into the Red Sea it was reported to the Patra's master, Captain Mohammed Shaaban, that there was a fire in the engine room and that the flames were spreading rapidly through the ship. Shaaban ordered the *Patra* to be abandoned and sent out an SOS.

Many passengers refused to get into the ship's lifeboats without their belongings, which they had been told to leave behind, until they were forced to do so by crew members carrying axes. A Soviet tanker, *Lenino*, along with several other vessels headed towards the *Patra* and were able to save 201 passengers and crew. Another 100 perished and the vessel finally sank. Investigators concluded that the fire had been caused by a gas leak from an engine.

Below: The Danish ferry Kronprins Frederik, *which was later renamed the* Patra. *The ship was working as a roll-on, roll-off ferry when it was destroyed by fire in 1976.*

90

AMOCO CADIZ, ENGLISH CHANNEL

MARCH 16, 1978

The *Torrey Canyon* oil spillage of March 1976 was still fresh in many people's minds when, less than two years later, disaster struck the supertanker *Amoco Cadiz* as it was making its way fully laden from the Persian Gulf to Rotterdam. The 288,513-ton supertanker sailed under the Liberian flag and was carrying around 250,000 tons of heavy crude oil. The tanker never completed its journey.

The *Amoco Cadiz* negotiated the Cape of Good Hope (it was far too large to be able to sail through the Suez canal) and then sailed up the coast of Africa without encountering any problems. As the tanker headed up the west coast of France, it approached a congested area of sea some 30 miles (48km) off the northern tip of Brittany. Beyond lay the busy waters of the English Channel. Regulations were in place here so that both north and south bound shipping had to stick to their own channels. This so-called "traffic separation" scheme was intended to prevent collisions.

The *Amoco Cadiz* entered the zone at a time of year when gales are common and can be ferocious. A supertanker under power should have been able to cope with the conditions, however. On the morning of March 16 the *Amoco Cadiz* had to maneuver to enter the northbound channel of the separation scheme. Shortly before 1000 hours the vessel's steering gear suffered a total failure – the rudder jammed hard to port. The tanker's master, Captain Pasquali Bardari, reacted quickly. He stopped the tanker's engines, hoisted a "not under control" signal, and sent out a radio signal to warn other vessels of the danger.

A German salvage tug, the *Pacific*, heard Bardari's distress call and hurried to offer help. However, Bardari had a problem – he needed to contact a senior official from the ship's owners in Chicago for permission to accept a tow. It was the middle of the night in

Below: The supertanker Amoco Cadiz *wrecked on the rocks off the Brittany coast.*

Right: The
Amoco Cadiz
*broke in two a few
days after going
aground. Here the
wreck is seen
awash in a sea of
its own black oil.*

Chicago and permission was not given until 1545 hours. The first tow rope from the *Pacific* broke and a second, attached to the stern, failed to halt the *Amoco Cadiz*'s drift. Even its own anchors failed to stop the ship. At 2100 hours the tanker ran aground off the coast of Brittany. It was high tide and as the sea ebbed the vessel settled on to the rocks with its hull holed.

Crude oil poured out of the *Amoco Cadiz* for months. Despite the efforts of various agencies, deter-gents and booms failed to staunch the flow of oil. By March 19 the slick stretched for nearly 20 miles (32km). The French resorted to bombing the wreck, which by this time had broken in two. But by the time the *Amoco Cadiz* was swept away in a storm in March 1979, it had leaked over 250,000 tonnes of crude oil. Rough seas did, in fact, contribute to the dispersal of the oil. But not before the coastline of Brittany and its wildlife had been devastated.

*Right: Cleaning
up operations
begin on the beach
of the little port of
Portsall, Brittany.
It was to be many
months before
the coastline
of Brittany
recovered from
the disaster.*

OCEANOS, INDIAN OCEAN

AUGUST 4, 1991

Left: The last moments of the Greek liner Oceanos, *as it sinks in heavy seas off the coast of South Africa on August 4, 1991.*

The Greek-owned liner *Oceanos* had a long career during which it underwent several name changes. Originally called the *Jean Laborde*, the vessel was built in 1951 for France's Messageries Maritimes, and started in service carrying passengers and cargo between France and its African colonies. After going through several other owners, the vessel was bought by the Greek Epirotiki Lines in mid-1976 and was refitted to cater for the blossoming luxury cruise market, plying at first among the Greek islands. Some 500 passengers could be accommodated in the liner's well-appointed cabins.

The *Oceanos*'s date with destiny came during a charter cruise between East London and Durban in South Africa. On August 3, 1991, as the ship was negotiating high winds and rough seas, the captain was informed that his ship had sprung a leak in its engine room. There was a sudden power failure and it became clear that the *Oceanos* was foundering. The captain took the opportunity to abandon his ship and its passengers, supposedly to get ashore to coordinate the rescue effort. Amazingly, it was left to entertainers on board the ship to oversee the rescue. Remarkably – under the circumstances – there were no fatalities.

The evacuation, spearheaded by more than a dozen South African helicopters, was carried out smoothly and efficiently on August 4. All 580 people on board were taken off safely, the last few being removed with the aid of a Dutch container ship. The loss of the *Oceanos* – it finally slid beneath the waves bow-first in the afternoon – and the captain's behavior were a severe embarrassment to the Greek owners.

ESTONIA, BALTIC SEA

SEPTEMBER 28, 1994

The *Estonia* was a large, deep-sea ferry designed for service in the Baltic Sea. It had a speed of 21 knots and could carry 2000 passengers with berths for a little over half of them. Built in Germany during the early 1980s, the vessel was originally known as the *Viking Sally* and was operated between Stockholm, Mariehamm, and Abo by Sally Lines. The ferry had two owners in the early 1990s – and two different names – before being sold on to Estonian Steamship Lines in 1992. Two years later, the *Estonia* grabbed world headlines when it went down with a horrifying loss of life. It was the worst deep-sea ferry disaster yet seen.

The Estonian Steamship Lines, a joint enterprise between the Estonian government and a Swedish company, put the *Estonia* to work on the route between Tallin, the Estonian capital, and Stockholm.

The *Estonia*'s final voyage began at 1900 hours on September 27. The ferry sailed out from Tallin but there were worrying questions over the safety of its bow doors. An inspection conducted shortly before its departure found problems with their seals, which were supposed to ensure that the doors were watertight.

Less than 90 minutes out into the Baltic, the *Estonia* encountered severe weather. Some passengers retired

Above: The passenger and car ferry Estonia, *moored in Stockholm, Sweden. Two years after being bought by Estline, the ferry went down in the Baltic with the loss of more than 850 lives.*

Left: A rescue helicopter hovers above an upturned lifeboat from the Estonia *as it searches for survivors from the ferry.*

to their cabins to sleep; others stayed in the ship's more public areas. These decisions were destined to be of crucial importance as to who would or would not survive. Around midnight an engineer on a routine inspection found water gushing in through the bow doors. The vessel's pumps were operated and began to remove the water. But so great was the volume of water entering the cargo deck that the pumps could not cope. The *Estonia* was being swamped.

At 0124 hours the *Estonia* sent out a distress signal. The waterlogged ship, buffeted by high winds and raging seas, was listing dangerously. The vessel's engines then failed. Shortly before 0200 hours the *Estonia* rolled over and sank rapidly. Those who had opted to go to bed in their cabins had no chance of escape. Those who had decided to remain in the lounge areas had a slightly better chance of survival. But there was panic on board as people fought to get off the ship.

Some people were probably crushed by heavy furnishings or by fellow passengers scrambling over

them. Some did escape but few were able to reach the safety of the lifeboats. Most of those who ended up in the icy Baltic succumbed to exposure or were drowned.

Rescue vessels knew that the *Estonia* had foundered off the coast of Turku and the first to arrive reached the spot little more than 60 minutes after receiving the distress call. It was pitch black and the seas were mountainous, yet some people were rescued. Most of these were men who probably had greater reserves of strength to cope with the cold and heavy seas. However, more than 850 passengers and crew – the final tally may never be known – were lost.

The final resting place of the *Estonia* was discovered three days later and the scene videotaped. The vessel lay in 250 feet (80m) of water and its bow door had been sheared off, probably by the violence of the storm it encountered.

A report published over three years later concluded that the ferry's bow door had a weak locking system and the heavy seas had jolted the door open.

Above: Finnish Coast Guards carry the body of a victim ashore on the small island of Uto in the Baltic.

INDEX